D1550416

Joyous SEXUALITY

HEALING FROM THE EFFECTS OF FAMILY SEXUAL DYSFUNCTION

MIC HUNTER, M.S.

CompCare® Publishers
2415 Annapolis Lane
Minneapolis, MN 55441

Library of Congress Cataloging-in-Publication Data

Hunter, Mic.

Joyous sexuality: healing from the effects of family sexual dysfunction: a workbook/ Mic Hunter.

p. cm.

Includes bibliographical references.

ISBN 0-89638-271-0

1. Adult children of sex addicts—Rehabilitation. 2. Adult children of dysfunctional families—Rehabilitation. 3. Adult children of dysfunctional families—Behavior. 4. Adult child sexual abuse victims—Rehabilitation. 5. Psychosexual disorders. 6. Adult Children of Sexual Dysfunction (Group) 7. Twelve-step programs. I. Title.

RCX569.5.A32H86 1992
616.85'83—dc20   92-13587
                                                      CIP

Cover design by MacLean and Tuminelly

Inquiries, orders, and catalog requests should be addressed to:

CompCare Publishers
2415 Annapolis Lane
Minneapolis, Minnesota 55441

Call 612/559-4800 or
toll-free 800/328-3330

6   5   4   3   2   1

97   96   95   94   93   92

*To Karen, Rob, and Jody
for having the courage to start,
and stay in,
Adult Children of Sexual Dysfunction.*

Contents

THREE

FOUR

FIVE

Acknowledgments

Like so many things in my life, this book is the result of group effort. I am grateful to the following people for reviewing the first draft of my work: Rob, Karen, Jody, Teresa, Gail, Janet, and my dear friend, Steve. They made numerous important contributions to what you will read. Jane R. Thomas, my editor, helped me find the words to express what I meant. Finally, as always, I must mention Kate An, the person who stands by me through it all. I don't know what would have become of me without her.

Preface

A recovery movement is growing in America. People throughout the country are coming together in small groups to help one another heal from painful childhoods. This simple act is changing their lives. In the last dozen years I have been honored to watch several hundred such people turn their lives around. Their faces passed through my awareness as I wrote this book. I cannot describe the effect that knowing them has had on my life. I would not be the person I am now were it not for them, the things they said, and the things they did not say.

One such group is Adult Children of Sexual Dysfunction (ACSD). This self-help group formed in Minneapolis, Minnesota, on January 21, 1988. It is based on the Twelve Steps and Twelve Traditions of Alcoholics Anonymous. The membership continues to grow, and meetings have started in other cities as well. As you read through the text of the book you will see reference to the Characteristics (pp. 7–8) and Promises (p. 78) written by the members of ACSD. In fact, the main title of this book is a phrase taken from the ACSD Promises.

In the back of the book are some of the findings from a 1990 survey of ACSD members. I have included this information because many people from dysfunctional families have a sense of being isolated or different from other people. Learning that other people have had similar experiences and have responded with nearly identical attitudes and behaviors can help reduce the sense of not being normal. If the people who came before you could heal from the injuries of the past, so can you.

At various points in the book you will be encouraged to reflect on ways the material applies to your life. A series of questions will be posed. You will gain more understanding of yourself if you go slowly and actually write out a response to each question. Although that process will be painful, it also will be rewarding. The more you understand how you came to be the way you are, the more easily you will make the changes you have sought.

One day while I was working on the manuscript for this book I was in an airplane, seated beside a woman who was reading a self-help book about communication. At one point, we each took a break from our tasks. I asked to look through the book she was reading. It contained numerous exercises that the reader was encouraged to complete before moving on to the next chapter. She said she had not attempted these exercises, or the suggestions in dozens of other self-help books she had read. I asked her whether her life had improved since she started to read self-help books. She said sadly that none had made a profound impact on her life. I told her I was sure that none would, at least not the way she was using them. Insight alone is not enough to enable anyone to change; action is required. I hope that this book will help you take the action necessary for a full and serene life.

What Is Family Sexual Dysfunction?

When anything is functioning well, it is performing as required, working properly. A fully functional family is able effectively and efficiently to meet the physical, emotional, spiritual, and sexual needs of all of its members. The children in a healthy family receive active, nurturing, respectful parenting from the adults who give them accurate and useful information about the world and teach them to behave appropriately. Such a child goes out into the world knowing how to interact with other people in a manner that makes it likely that her needs will be met.

In contrast, a dysfunctional family does not accomplish what a family is expected to do. That ineffectiveness does *not* mean that there are no good times, that people hurt each other on purpose, that nobody loves anybody, or that somebody planned the family's dysfunction.

Human behavior tends to fall along a continuum. At one end of the range, behavior is excessive; there is too much of it. On the opposite end, problems arise because there is too little of a needed behavior. A family that thinks and behaves in extremes is a dysfunctional family. The extreme style of thinking and behaving prevents family members from fulfilling their needs in a reasonable fashion. In a sexually dysfunctional family something is going on that negatively affects the sexuality of the family members. They end up being hurt by sexuality instead of enjoying it. The dysfunction in the family system can be compounded by sexual dysfunction within the society and culture that has been passed on from generation to generation and become traditional.

Three basic extremes are common in sexually dysfunctional families: the overvaluation of sex, negative attitudes about sex, and sexual shutdown. Abuse may occur in all three types of families. The term *family* means different things to different people. For one person, it might conjure up the image of people who all live in one house. For someone else, a family is several generations of people. Others' definition includes all of the people, related or not, who took part in important events or had a significant impact on their lives. Birth parents, stepparents, adoptive parents, foster parents, grandparents, and other guardians may have played a role in your upbringing. You are free to determine what constitutes your family and to think about those people when you are asked to think about your childhood.

The Family That Overvalues Sex

In these families, sex is the most important thing in life. A constant sexual tension or energy hangs in the air. Sexuality becomes the predominant focus of most interactions. Sex is a preoccupation through which everything is viewed. Humor is sexual. Family members are seen as sex objects. A person's worth is based on sexual attractiveness. The more sex partners one has or the higher the frequency of sexual behavior, the more important the person is considered.

In this type of family, people experience sex as the primary method of coping with life. They sexualize their emotions. Instead of feeling lonely, they feel "horny." When sad or hurt, rather than look for comforting, they think they need sex. Faced with an emotional situation, they experience a compulsive urge to be sexual. Emotions are not appropriately expressed but are "acted out" sexually. Some people refer to this behavior pattern as sex addiction. There is a great deal of controversy about the label *sex addiction*. Some people prefer the term *compulsive sexual behavior*. Others say that arguments over terminology are pointless, since the problem does not even exist. I will assume the existence of the condition and will use both terms throughout the book. The use of an addictions model does not excuse anyone's behavior. People still need to be held accountable for what they did or did not do, regardless of what term one uses to describe the problem.

Families that overvalue sex view it not only as an important element of life but as a powerful one as well, since they perceive it to be the force that drives people. Many members of the mutual-help fellowship, Adult Children of Sexual Dysfunction (ACSD), report that there was at least one sexually compulsive member in their families. (The Appendix contains the statistics gathered in a survey of ACSD membership. ACSD's address appears in the Resources section.) The children in these families are sometimes encouraged to date and to be sexual before they are ready. They may be expected to wear overly revealing clothes or adult-style clothing and make-up, even when they are very young. They frequently are exposed to pornography and to adults talking in detail about sex.

Other forms of sexualized abuse occur in families that overvalue sex. An adult may try to touch a child or ask him to touch the adult in a sexual manner. An adult may take part in household voyeurism, arranging to view the child nude. This behavior ranges from walking in on the child when he is dressing or bathing to drilling peepholes in bedroom walls.

Some adults expose their sexual organs to children in order to become sexually excited. Their methods vary. Some are obvious, such as masturbating or having intercourse where a child can see or hear them. Others are less obvious—wearing a skirt or shorts with no underwear, for example, and sitting in such a way that the child can easily see the adult's genitals, or wearing see-through nightgowns in the presence of the child. (For more information on sex addiction and sexual abuse, see the bibliography.)

Sexual abuse is not the only possible harm caused by sexually compulsive parents. They are likely to put more time and energy into their relationship with sex than they give their relationship with their children. As a result, the children of sexually addicted parents have stories very similar to those of children whose parents are addicted to alcohol and other drugs. Broken promises, missed appointments, and unexplained absences are these children's common experience. Even the parent who is physically present may be mentally or emotionally absent. A person who is compulsive about anything in life is, by definition, preoccupied with it. This focus prevents the ability to be mentally engaged with others, because the addict is constantly entertaining thoughts about the addiction. Even when sex is not in the forefront, the parent may be preoccupied with shame and guilt about the sexual behavior she is participating in or the lies she has told to hide her actions.

The Family That Is Negative about Sex

Like families that overvalue sex, sex-negative families see it as a very powerful force. They, too, are sexually preoccupied, but they focus on ensuring that sexuality be avoided and repressed. Sex is something to be feared, because it is seen to be dangerous, perhaps even evil. These families frequently enforce rigid rules about sexual behavior, intended to prevent people from being sexual and, sometimes, from even thinking sexual thoughts. Usually these rules are narrow and punitive. When a person violates one of the family's expectations about sexuality, he feels ashamed, as if he were an unworthy person. (Notice that I said *when* a person violates the expectations, not *if*. The rules are usually so narrow that it is impossible not to violate them. Merely having a sexual thought or noticing that someone is physically attractive is viewed as having a "filthy mind.")

Sometimes religion justifies these families' beliefs about sexuality with doctrines that assert God's disapproval of sex and the human body. Since the topic of sex is viewed as disgusting, the children in these families are not free to ask questions about sexuality and reproduction. If the children are told any of the "facts of life," they usually hear only a description of the body's "plumbing," possibly accompanied by a lecture on the evils of sex. Like those that overvalue sex, these families maintain an active, extreme, and sexualized focus on physical appearance. Children often are required to cover their bodies at all times. Even in very warm weather they are expected to cover themselves completely. As teenagers, they are not allowed to date or otherwise socialize with peers of the other gender because something sexual might happen. They never learn how to interact with other people their own age and gain social skills necessary to healthy adult functioning.

Family histories frequently show that family sexual styles skip generations. If one generation was overly focused on sex, the children of that family become sex-negative adults and raise their children in that mode. When the third generation become adults, they reject the rigidity of their parents but go to the other extreme, becoming sexually compulsive.

The Sexually Shut-down Family

Even though it is not a preoccupation in the sexually shut-down family, sex is just as dysfunctional in this kind of family as it is in the first two types. The topic is not merely ignored, as if there were a lack of interest in it; there is a nearly phobic response. All references to the subject are absent. People actively work to suppress awareness of sexuality. They may wear clothing that is unattractive or that hides the shape of their bodies. They never discuss where babies come from. Children's sexual development is ignored; when secondary sexual characteristics appear, such as enlarging breasts, menstruation, or development of facial or pubic hair, the family members pretend not to notice and do not talk about the changes.

The Family That Combines Dysfunctional Styles

Some families combine the three inadequate styles. One adult may overvalue sex, while the other is negative about sex or shut down. Their children are caught in the middle, receiving conflicting messages about what to believe about sexuality.

When I walk at the small city zoo near my house, I observe people's responses to the animals' sexual behavior. Parents who overvalue sex insist upon staying to watch the animals long after their child has become bored and wants to see something else. Parents who are sex-negative either cover their child's eyes and flee or stay to watch, remarking about the disgusting sight and declaring that the zoo ought to prevent such outrageous occurrences. The shut-down family tries to ignore the behavior. If they wander by and the child notices what is happening or asks a question, the parents pretend that they don't know what the child is asking about.

Fortunately a few parents realize that sex is a natural part of the lives of all animals, including humans. When a child comments on the zoo animals' copulating or masturbating, the parents matter-of-factly validate the reality of his observation.

Now that you have learned about the various types of family sexual dysfunction it will be useful for you to pause and think about how this information applies to your life. A series of questions will facilitate this process. You will gain more if you actually write a response to the questions. It may be painful, but you will gain insights that will help in your recovery.

Which type of family style did you experience when you were growing up?

_____

What experience from your past came to mind as you read the section on the family style that best fit your family?

_____

_____

_____

_____

_____

_____

_____

_____

_____

_____

Characteristics of Sexually Dysfunctional Families

The members of ACSD have identified characteristics that were common in their families when they were young. (See the Appendix for further information about the survey from which these characteristics are quoted.) Of course, not every family had every characteristic, and even those families that exhibited a specific characteristic did not all manifest it to the same degree. What matters is *not* how many dysfunctional characteristics a family displayed or even how severe any one characteristic was, but the effect that family sexual dysfunction had on its members. Unfortunately, painful early events shape attitudes about self and others. These attitudes or mental habits affect a person's behavior. The next section focuses on identifying the characteristics commonly found in sexually dysfunctional families and contrasts them with healthy sexuality.

Some Characteristics of Adult Children of Sexual Dysfunction

1. Many of us were given harmful information about sex instead of appropriate, accurate, or useful information about sex.

2. Many of us experienced shame or confusion about our bodies, our gender, and our sexuality.

3. Many of us grew up in families in which sex tended to be viewed in extremes: Sex was all important and/or sex was dirty, disgusting, or naughty.

4. Many of us grew up in families in which disrespectful behaviors or remarks about gender and sexuality were common.

5. Many of us grew up in families in which there was a lack of nourishing touch.

6. As adults, many of us experienced confusion, discomfort, or terror in the face of sexuality.

7. As adults, many of us experienced difficulties in establishing intimate relationships.

8. As adults, many of us experienced fear or shame when we acted in healthy sexual ways.

9. As adults, many of us misidentified the roles of sex in relationships, attempting to use sex to avoid abandonment, control others, or fill our emptiness.

10. As adults, many of us confused sex with emotional intimacy.

Characteristic One: Harmful Information

Many of us were given harmful information about sex instead of appropriate, accurate, or useful information about sex.

Everyone who grows up in America has access to information about sex. We are surrounded by sexual messages in popular music lyrics, in films, and on television, the covers of magazines at checkout counters, and billboards. We also learn about sex by watching how our parents and other family members interact. If you saw your mother push your father away from her when he tried to kiss her, you were learning something about sex and sex roles. We learn by listening to what others say or don't say about sex. If they mention it in only a joking manner, then you learn that sex is not to be taken seriously. If they treat it only in a negative way, you learn that sex is bad. If they never mention sex, you learn that it is unmentionable and therefore bad.

Some people get a more formal education in the classroom. When I was sixteen years old, for example, half of my high school class took a sex education course during the first semester, while the other half ("the lucky ones," we thought) took driver's education so they could get their driver's licenses. After the school year ended, I was struck by how similar sex education and driver's training had been. Students learned to drive primarily by watching films about the victims of automobile accidents; the sex education class presented the view that sex leads only to unwanted children and venereal disease. There was no discussion of emotions, values, or the reasons people engage in sexual behavior. We heard nothing about the possible joys of sexuality.

Some adult children from sexually dysfunctional families are very sexually active. In fact, they even may be sexually compulsive. However, a person's high level of sexual activity does not necessarily imply that she possesses accurate or useful information about sex. In dysfunctional families, the adults themselves may not have accurate sexual information to give the children. Even if the parents do have knowledge of sexual matters, they may be too ashamed to talk to their child.

Incorrect, insufficient, or distorted information harms children in various ways. When facts are withheld about sexuality and other functions of the human body, the child gets the message that these topics are so horrible, so shameful, that they can't even be mentioned. If children cannot safely ask about their bodies, they remain ignorant and have to make up their own, naive explanations. Unfortunately many people carry an inaccurate understanding of sex into their adulthood.

Inaccurate information also impairs children. A parent may unknowingly pass on incorrect information or actually may lie, saying something he knows to be false. In either situation,

9

the misinformation is damaging because the child goes into the world unprepared.

Inappropriate information about sex is a third way parents' statements injure children. A parent who tells a child about sexual frustration in the parent's marriage, for example, is burdening her with information she neither needs nor understands. She is being asked to act as marriage counselor and sex therapist for her parents, a reversal of parent-child roles. Rather than the adult taking care of the child, the child is caring for the adult. Another example is the mother who tells her child graphic details of her sexual history and sexual fantasies. It is the parents' responsibility to help the child, not the other way around.

Useless information also does children harm. For example, when a very young child asks for the first time "Where do babies come from?" and is told much more than he can comprehend, the facts are bewildering. "Well, you see dear, during copulation the man ejaculates seminal fluid into the woman's vagina. The spermatozoa contained in the seminal fluid make their way up the Fallopian tube toward the ovum...." All of this is *accurate*, but it is *not useful* to a child. For the information to be useful, the child has to be able to grasp the concepts. A child ought to be told about sexual matters throughout life, in terms that are appropriate to his age. The older he gets, the more detailed the information may be. Unfortunately, many parents deliver the "facts of life" talk only once and never discuss the topic again.

Now is an appropriate time to reflect on the type of information you were given about sexual matters. In order to help you personalize and apply the information you have already read, answer the following questions.

Where and from whom have you received *formal* information about sex and sexuality, such as a sex education class?

What *helpful* messages about sex and sexuality did you receive?

_____

_____

_____

_____

_____

_____

_____

_____

What *harmful* messages about sex and sexuality did you receive?

_____

_____

_____

_____

_____

_____

_____

_____

Did your parents provide you with a "where babies come from" talk? If so, what did they tell you? How did you feel when they told you?

_____

_____

_____

_____

_____

_____

_____

_____

What, if anything, was said about masturbation by your family?

_____

_____

_____

_____

Was birth control discussed by your family?

_____

_____

_____

_____

How did your family react when your body began to change at puberty?

_____

_____

_____

_____

_____

_____

_____

Whom, if anyone, did you talk to about your first wet dream or menstrual period? What did you say, and how did the other person respond?

_____

_____

_____

_____

_____

_____

_____

How was dating discussed by your family?

_____

_____

_____

_____

_____

_____

_____

_____

What *helpful* messages about sex and sexuality did you receive from your family?

_____

_____

_____

_____

_____

_____

_____

What *harmful* messages about sex and sexuality did you receive from your family?

_____

_____

_____

_____

_____

_____

_____

_____

Where and from whom have you received *informal* information about sex and sexuality (for example, locker room talks, watching people interact)?

_____

_____

_____

_____

_____

_____

_____

_____

What *helpful* messages about sex and sexuality did you receive?

_____

_____

_____

_____

_____

_____

_____

_____

_____

What *harmful* messages about sex and sexuality did you receive?

_____

_____

_____

_____

_____

_____

_____

_____

How have you been influenced by the media (television, music, films, books, magazines, pornography) in matters of sex, sexuality, and relationships?

What *helpful* messages about sex and sexuality did you receive from the media?

What *harmful* messages about sex and sexuality did you receive from the media?

_____

_____

_____

_____

_____

_____

_____

_____

_____

Write a list of topics related to sex and sexuality that you would like more information about.

_____

_____

_____

Choose a date by which you will have obtained books or talked with someone who will give you the information you are seeking. Write that date here.

_____

_____

_____

Characteristic Two: Misperceptions

Many of us experienced shame or confusion about our bodies, our gender, and our sexuality.

The Second Characteristic common among ACSD members is a logical consequence of the First. If a person does not have appropriate, accurate, or useful information about sex, confusion necessarily follows. Ninety-six percent of the members of ACSD reported that this statement definitely applied to them, and the rest said that it was somewhat apt.

This Second Characteristic, which focuses on confusion, may itself be confusing for some people. Therefore, some definitions are in order. The word *bodies* is fairly clear. It refers to your physical person, how you actually appear to others. It also refers to your body image, how you *think* you appear to others, your mental picture of yourself. Many people who came from sexually dysfunctional families have distorted body images. They think they are fat or skinny or ugly, even though those around them would use none of these words to describe them.

A person's body image may have very little to do with reality. I have had several clients who made their living as highly paid professional models. Day after day they were paid huge sums to pose for photographs that appeared on the covers of magazines. Despite evidence to the contrary, they thought of themselves as ugly and deformed. They could not comprehend why anyone would want to photograph them, let alone pay them for it. They assumed that any day they would be discovered for the ugly persons they truly were, and their careers would suddenly end in humiliation.

People who once were obese sometimes hold on to the belief that they are fat long after they have lost the excessive weight. Anorexia nervosa is an extreme example of a distorted body image. A person who suffers from this disorder literally starves herself to death, all the while seeing herself as too fat.

Gender is the second term mentioned in Characteristic Two that causes confusion in people from sexually dysfunctional families. It refers to the identity and roles associated with being male or female. More than simply whether you have male or female sex organs, the word *gender* refers to how you express your being male or female. Sex is biologically determined. People learn gender by watching others to see how they act. If you want to know whether you are a man or a woman you can determine the answer by looking at your body. But to know whether you are a "real" man or woman you must look into your definitions of masculinity and femininity for your answer. That is a gender question, not a sex question.

Sexuality is the third area that must be defined to gain a full understanding of the Second Characteristic. One aspect of sexuality is sexual behavior, physical acts. Sexual orientation is another aspect of sexuality. Some people have same-sex orientations. Other people are attracted only to the other sex. Still others are able to express their sexuality with people of either sex.

At this point, respond to the following questions to see how you can reduce some of the shame and confusion you experience around the three areas mentioned in Characteristic Two.

When you think about someone looking at your body, how do you feel, and what do you think that person is thinking about the way you look?

_____

_____

_____

_____

_____

_____

_____

_____

Look in a mirror at your body. (A full-length mirror is best if you have one.) How do you feel as you look at yourself?

_____

_____

_____

_____

_____

_____

_____

_____

Remove as much of your clothing as you are comfortable with and look again at your body. What reactions do you have?

_____

_____

_____

_____

_____

_____

_____

_____

Which parts of your body are you comfortable looking at?

_____

_____

_____

_____

Which parts of your body are you *un*comfortable looking at?

_____

_____

_____

_____

What thoughts and emotions do you have as you look at these parts?

_____

_____

_____

_____

_____

_____

_____

_____

_____

Is there someone trustworthy you could ask to offer an opinion about your appearance? If so, write what they say.

_____

_____

_____

_____

_____

_____

_____

_____

When you think about your gender, how do you feel?

_____

_____

_____

_____

_____

_____

_____

_____

When you think about the other gender, how do you feel?

_____

_____

_____

_____

_____

_____

_____

_____

Do you believe that one gender is better than the other? If so, how did you come to this belief?

_____

_____

_____

_____

_____

_____

_____

_____

_____

Do you worry that you are not a "real" man or woman? If so, how can you answer this question to your satisfaction?

_____

_____

_____

_____

_____

_____

_____

_____

Is there someone you can trust whose opinion you could ask concerning your masculinity or femininity? If so, write what you learn from that person.

_____

_____

_____

_____

_____

_____

_____

_____

When you think of expressing your sexuality, how do you feel?

_____

_____

_____

_____

_____

_____

_____

Characteristic Three: Extreme Views

Many of us grew up in families in which sex tended to be viewed in extremes: Sex was all important and/or sex was dirty, disgusting, or naughty.

In families that overvalue sex, it is all-important. In families that are negative about sex, it is dirty, disgusting, or naughty. Some families view sex simultaneously in both of these extreme ways. Such a situation creates a double-bind. Take the admonition, "Sex is dirty and disgusting; save it for the one you love." In most cases, the two contradictory messages are divided so that the double-bind is not so obvious. A person in a double-bind is in a no-win situation. Whatever she does seems wrong. People who have lived with many double-binds end up believing they can't do anything right.

A client who had grown up in such circumstances explained to me how the double-bind worked in his family. When he was a child, his mother used to tell him that women liked sex. Whenever his father touched her, however, she exclaimed, "Get away from me, you dirty old man. Men want women for only one thing." My client carried these lessons with him into his adult relationships. When he asked his partner to be sexual with him and she said no, he felt ashamed. "She's right to refuse me," he thought. "I'm a pervert for asking her to do that in the first place."

When his partner said she wanted to be sexual with him, he felt ashamed again. "She is just having sex with me because she thinks it is her duty," he thought. "She is only pretending she likes sex. She really doesn't want to be doing this. I had better hurry up and get it over with." In his recovery, he began to see that he was assuming what his partner was thinking, based on his impossible childhood family rules about sex. Once he began to talk about sexuality with his partner, he began to learn that she did not share his beliefs about the horrors of sex.

Recovery from the effects of families' extreme attitudes (Characteristic Three) involves putting sex in perspective. It is neither the reason for living nor the root of all evil, but merely another natural part of life, like eating and sleeping. Whether eating or sleeping are appropriate depends on the time and place. The same is true of sex. John Brantner, a former teacher at the University of Minnesota, humorously compared sex to peanut butter: "It is enjoyed by people of all ages; it is not very good by itself; if you get too much, it can be a real mess; it comes in many different styles, but it is really all the same; and, if it is not taken care of, then it goes bad."

Since recovery involves seeing sex temperately, as merely one element in a balanced life, you will want to define healthy sexual values for yourself.

Write some positive words or phrases to describe how you view sex or how you wish to view it (as playful, safe, honest, respectful, spontaneous, spiritual, silly, intimate, rambunctious, pleasurable, relaxed, exciting, guilt-free, shame-free, gentle, cheerful, frisky, festive, and so on).

As a reminder of what sex can become for you, make a sign with some of these terms on it and place it where you will see it when you are sexual.

Characteristic Four: Disrespect

Many of us grew up in families in which disrespectful behaviors or remarks about gender and sexuality were common.

Some disrespectful remarks are more obvious than others. For example, a man I worked with told me that when he sat with his mother on the beach when he was a boy, she made disparaging remarks about the boys and men who walked by. "I wish men would cover themselves," she always said. "Their bodies are so ugly. It is disgusting to have to see them." Not surprisingly, he grew into a man who thought of himself as ugly. He could not imagine that another person might enjoy seeing his body, let alone touching him.

Another man, a client, remembered dating a girl in high school who invited him to supper with her family. During the meal her father asked him, "Don't you think my daughter would be sexier if she had bigger boobs?" Apparently she had grown so accustomed to such remarks that she did not appear embarrassed. My client, on the other hand, was speechless.

In some families, sexual terms are used to punish the children. Think of how many common insults include sexual terms. A child who hears comments such as "You little prick" or "You're nothing but a whore" is learning several things. First, he concludes that he is a bad person. Associating sex with being bad, he assumes that it is a bad thing in itself.

The disrespectful remarks about sexuality that many people hear growing up come in the form of humor, a very powerful form of communication. A person discloses attitudes about such important matters as religion, politics, and sex through the jokes she thinks are funny. Some families talk about sexuality only when they tell jokes. Serious discussions of sexuality do not come up. No one has any means of addressing sexual concerns without the risk of being laughed at. Sometimes the jokes are general ("Did you hear the one about the...?"), but family members themselves may also be the focus of the jokes. They may be laughed at for merely being male or female, for developing facial hair or breasts, or for developing differently from their peers. It is difficult to complain, even though the comments are hurtful, because they are packaged in the form of humor. If the butt of family humor protests that he does not like what is being said, then he is accused of not being able to take a joke.

Heterosexism is another common form of disrespect, like racism, sexism, classism, or materialism. Like the racists who believe that they are better than members of other races, heterosexist people believe that heterosexuals are better people than homosexuals or bisexuals. Unfortunately we live in a heterosexist society, so we are surrounded by disrespectful remarks, jokes, stereotypes, and insults such as "fairy," "dyke," "lezzie," "faggot," and "queer." This pervasive disparagement makes it very difficult for homosexual and bisexual people to celebrate their sexuality comfortably. This dynamic is important, since 22 percent of the membership of the ACSD groups studied identified themselves as bisexual and 8 percent were homosexual.

Now take some time to reflect on the behaviors and remarks related to gender and sexuality you witnessed while growing up in your family. Respond to the following questions.

What remarks about gender did you hear?

What effect did these remarks have on your view of *your gender*?

_____

_____

_____

_____

_____

_____

_____

_____

What effect did these remarks have on your view of the *other gender*?

_____

_____

_____

_____

_____

_____

_____

What remarks about sexuality did you hear growing up?

_____

_____

_____

_____

_____

_____

_____

What effect did these remarks have on your view of *your* sexuality?

_____

_____

_____

_____

_____

_____

_____

What kinds of remarks about gender and sexuality would you like to have heard? Write them here.

_____

_____

_____

_____

_____

_____

_____

How would your life be different now, if you had heard these remarks when you were growing up?

_____

_____

_____

_____

_____

_____

_____

Reread these positive remarks each day, either aloud or silently, for one month. At the end of the time write the effect this exercise has had on your view of gender and sexuality.

Characteristic Five: Touch Deprivation

Many of us grew up in families in which there was a lack of nourishing touch.

Touch is a powerful gesture. It can comfort, and it can injure. Not surprisingly, when the topic of touch is discussed in an ACSD meeting, intense emotions are triggered. In some sexually dysfunctional families, the only way to obtain human touch is to take part in contact sports, such as wrestling or football. Otherwise, touch may be exclusively tickles or punches on the shoulder. Even if hugs are given, they tend to be the type that involve frantic slapping on the back or "bear hugs" rather than gentle, soothing holding. The only touch some families exchange is violent. These people touch one another only by pushing, shaking, slapping, punching, or pinching. Still other families provide no touch of any kind. People do not greet one another with a hug, a handshake, or any other contact. When a family member is in pain, nobody offers a shoulder to cry on or a hand to hold. An individual may experience the "double whammy," both abusive touch and deprivation of nourishing touch.

At the other extreme from families who never touch are the families who touch excessively. Family members incessantly stroke one another. They are constantly touching, and are governed by the unspoken rule that it is unacceptable to decline contact.

Touch is nurturing when it adds something positive to life. The word *nurture* comes from the Latin root of the word *nourish*. To nourish someone is to support, to comfort, to help the person grow. People who have experienced non-nourishing or exploitive touch describe it as "icky," "dirty," or "slimy." "I wanted to take a shower afterward," they say. Such contact, sometimes described as "hungry touch," takes something away from the other person.

Parents who themselves did not receive enough of the right sort of touch may turn to their children to fill this need and may even require that they provide back rubs, foot massages, hairbrushing, and companionship in bed. In my clinical practice, I have seen a pattern that alternates— one generation in a family witholding touch and the next generation hungry for it. The people who were deprived of touch as children become adults who try to heal the consequent wounds by touching their children excessively. When these children become adults, they avoid touching their own children in an effort to avoid smothering them.

Some children are required to hug or kiss adults whom they fear or do not know well. This demand confuses children. They have learned not to talk to strangers, yet they must open themselves up and unwillingly exchange hugs and kisses with visitors in their home. They are learning the damaging lesson that they cannot trust their emotions and their bodies are not their own.

A deprivation of nourishing touch also can be physically injurious. Babies who do not receive enough touch display such a typical pattern of response that it has been named "failure to thrive." Although these children have enough food to eat, the lack of human contact causes them to exhibit not only emotional problems but also poor *physical* development. They have low resistance to illness, poor intellectual skills, and a high rate of mortality. Lack of touch can be fatal. Adults and children who have been thus starved for touch often rock themselves when they are afraid, lonely, or ashamed. Comforting, safe touch can be emotionally and even physically painful to a person who has suffered years of isolation. Memories of being cut off from others flood back and seem overwhelming.

Some people whose childhood need for touch was neglected become adults who continue the pattern of neglect, rarely touching themselves to brush their hair or stroke their skin or rub their feet. Others go to the opposite extreme and constantly stimulate themselves. This pattern may become sexualized, as when one tries to satisfy the urge for touch by masturbation. It is no surprise that many members of ACSD (37 percent) describe themselves as "sexually addicted." People even may touch themselves in self-destructive ways, pulling their hair out, biting their nails or other parts of their bodies, or pinching, burning, or cutting themselves.

In some families that confuse physical intimacy with sexual intimacy, the parents withdraw *all* touch when the child reaches a certain age. Members of sexually dysfunctional families answer variously when asked at what age a child is too old to be touched. Some responses cite as early an age as four. On the contrary, I believe that humans are never too old to benefit from a safe, comforting touch from another person.

Sometimes touch is confusing or frightening because of a hidden agenda. For example, I have heard many stories from clients whose parents or siblings offered them back rubs. The offer seemed innocent enough, even kind, but the back rub threatened to become a breast rub or buttock rub. Deprived children may become so "hungry" for physical contact that they are vulnerable to sexual exploitation by others, both inside and outside the family. A neglected child tolerates sexual contact because it is the only available attention or touch. When ACSD was formed, 75 percent of the members reported a history of childhood sexual abuse.

Since touch is such a powerful issue, it is important that when you attend a mutual-help group meeting, seek psychotherapy, or otherwise interact with others, you are willing and able to set limits. If you do not want to hug someone (or anyone) for whatever reason, *it is your right* to decline the offer. Do not let anyone taunt you into accepting what you don't want. You are allowed to say no this week to a hug or touch even if you said yes last week.

At this point, take some time to think about the role touch has played in your life. These questions will help you to be more focused.

What experiences related to touch did you have as a child?

How did these events affect you?

As an adult, what role does touch play in your life?

How do you touch yourself?

_____

_____

_____

_____

_____

_____

_____

_____

How do you react now to being touched by others?

_____

_____

_____

_____

_____

_____

_____

_____

_____

Who, if anyone, is safe for you to touch and be touched by in your life?

_____

_____

_____

_____

_____

_____

_____

_____

Are there people who are touching you in a way you do not like? If so, what can you do to set limits so that you are only touched comfortably and by appropriate persons?

_____

_____

_____

_____

_____

_____

_____

_____

What can you do to improve the role of touch in your life?

CHAPTER THREE

Adult Child Issues

The first five Characteristics of ACSD describe the symptoms of sexually dysfunctional families. The remaining five present the adult consequences of a childhood spent in such circumstances.

Characteristic Six: Fear in Sexual Situations

As adults, many of us experienced confusion, discomfort, or terror in the face of sexuality.

It is not surprising that, with 75 percent of the members of ACSD reporting that they were sexually abused as children, they also would report confusion, discomfort, or terror in sexual situations. People who are frightened when sexual contact occurs may freeze physically and go numb emotionally. A person who cannot move or react allows the encounter to continue without protest. A respectful, attentive partner would likely notice the lack of response and ask what was going on. Most people do not desire sex with a partner who is frightened or emotionally absent.

Another response to fear is thinking about other things, which dampens one's mental awareness of present events. People describe this reaction as "spacing out" or "going away." People who have been physically or sexually abused often learn to absent themselves during assaults in order to cope with the trauma. This response persists in adulthood, however, when other, perhaps better, options are available, even when a sexual experience is not abusive.

One reason some people become confused in sexual situations is that they do not realize their entitlement to say no if they wish. "No": I remind my clients that this declaration is a complete sentence. There is no need for an explanation or justification. "I don't want to" is a completely satisfactory reason for declining sex. If you have said no, a respectful partner accepts your answer and does not pressure you to change your mind, punish you by withdrawing from the relationship, or continue to touch you in a sexual manner. If your partner does not respect your decision, then you are being mistreated.

In order to apply what you have read, respond to the following questions.

Describe a time when you felt confused concerning sexuality.

_____

_____

_____

_____

_____

_____

_____

_____

_____

_____

_____

What type of discomfort do you experience when you are being sexual?

_____

_____

_____

_____

_____

_____

_____

_____

_____

_____

What triggers terror for you in sexual situations?

_____

_____

_____

_____

_____

_____

If you are currently in a sexual relationship, is your partner doing things that confuse you or lead to your being uncomfortable or even terrified? If so, what is your partner doing? Do you think your partner would stop doing these things if you asked?

What will you do the next time you are in a sexual situation and experience confusion?

_____

_____

_____

_____

_____

_____

Discomfort?

_____

_____

_____

_____

_____

_____

Terror?

_____

_____

_____

_____

_____

Characteristic Seven: Difficulty with Intimacy

As adults, many of us experienced difficulties in establishing intimate relationships.

One hundred percent of ACSD members said that this statement definitely applies to them. In addition, it appears that they are less likely to marry and more likely to divorce than their neighbors (see the Appendix). In my experience, the primary factor that leads people to attend a support group like ACSD is a serious problem in relationships, either with others or with themselves. When you do not like yourself, it is difficult to have a decent relationship with yourself, let alone an intimate, satisfying relationship with someone else.

The good news is that membership in a support group with others who have had similar experiences can relieve the difficulty people have in establishing intimate relationships. The bad news is that people from sexually dysfunctional families find it hard to commit themselves completely to any group that presents the opportunity for emotional intimacy. The very idea frightens them. Even if they do attend meetings, some people are too intimidated to form meaningful relationships with others at the meetings. They are quiet during the group discussions of the Characteristics or Steps, avoid sharing personal matters during the check-in portion of the meeting, and do not use the phone lists to call others for support during the week.

Any person who joins a Twelve Step group does so not once, but many times; the level of intimacy increases with each new commitment. The first time you join is, of course, attendance at your first meeting. Merely by showing up, you are saying that you belong, that you are like other people. ACSD groups realize the courage of newcomers and may recognize it by awarding them a coin-size medallion imprinted with a slogan such as, "One day at a time," "Never alone again," or "Keep coming back."

As hard as it is to walk into the first meeting, many people report that the second meeting is even more difficult. The reason is that the first meeting likely triggered memories and emotions. In other words, you can attend your first meeting fairly naively, but, when you go back again, you know what you are getting into. Some people report that the better the experience at the initial meeting, the more difficult the next meeting becomes. People say, "They were all so friendly to me. I was welcomed right in. I hated it. I wanted to go there and be invisible." "They seemed to get along with each other so well," newcomers observe. They tell themselves, I'm sure they wouldn't like me once they got to know me. I'm sure my childhood experiences were much different [either not as bad or much worse] from the others', and they wouldn't be able to relate to me.

If attending the second meeting is the second level of joining, then the third level must be telling your story to the entire group. It is a highly intimate and powerful experience to relate your history to a group of people, particularly when they nod knowingly and even cry as you tell your family experiences. Since fear of intimacy is common among adult children from sexually dysfunctional families, it also is common for them suddenly to withdraw just as they begin to form emotionally close relationships with the other members.

This section has focused on intimacy. Consider the next series of questions in order to gain understanding of the role relationships play in your life today.

What relationship patterns have you noticed in your life?

_____

_____

_____

_____

_____

_____

_____

_____

Have you noticed any difference in the way you relate with men and with women? If so, write some examples.

_____

_____

_____

_____

_____

_____

_____

What do these differences tell you about your view of gender and sexuality?

_____

_____

_____

_____

_____

_____

_____

How are these patterns related to your childhood in a sexually dysfunctional family?

_____

_____

_____

_____

_____

_____

_____

_____

How do you respond to joining a group (a team, Twelve Step group, therapy group, party, or a new job)?

_____

_____

_____

_____

_____

_____

_____

_____

What are your strengths in relating to others?

What are your shortcomings in relating to others?

What steps can you take to reduce the effect of these shortcomings?

Characteristic Eight: Shame about Healthy Sexuality

As adults, many of us experienced fear or shame when we acted in healthy sexual ways.

Many paradoxes become evident in Twelve Step recovery. (The Twelve Steps and the Adapted Twelve Steps are on pages 76 and 77). One of these paradoxes is implicit in the First Step, "We admitted that we were powerless over sexual dysfunction—that our lives had become unmanageable." Not until you acknowledge your powerlessness are you able to gain power. Once you begin to accept your inability to manage events, your life begins to become more manageable. The Eighth Characteristic poses another paradox. It is contrary to common sense for people to do something healthy and then feel guilty, ashamed, or terrified. Yet some people from sexually dysfunctional families experience exactly that contradiction.

One reason for this reaction is that many people from dysfunctional families have learned to dissociate when they are in emotionally charged situations. They do so in order to cope with fear and shame; sex, particularly intimate, healthy sex, can be a highly charged experience. Dissociation is the process of "spacing out" or getting emotionally numb. A mild instance of dissociation occurs when someone who is saying something painful distances herself from it emotionally by speaking as if she were talking about someone other than herself.

"I came home from school early one day, looking forward to talking with my father," one of my clients told me. "I heard something that sounded like two people having sex, which confused me, since my mother was out of the country on a vacation. As I walked into the living room, I saw my father having sex with another woman. It was a really painful sight. You get angry when someone you love does something like that to you." Notice how the speaker used the word *I* until she began to describe her emotions. Then she began to say *you*.

When people begin recovery, frequently their need to dissociate diminishes. They begin to feel emotions in situations that used to be too threatening. Their awareness of more emotions may make them afraid, as if a powerful emotional response meant that something is wrong. Some people fear that their emotions will overwhelm them. Clients often say that their first sexual experience without dissociating is such a potent experience that they begin to weep. So here is another paradox: if you cry when you are having sex, you may just be getting healthier.

Adult children who grew up in the midst of any serious family dysfunction can only guess what constitutes normal behavior. Many clients ask me whether their sexual behavior and attitudes are normal, meaning usual or average. Unfortunately, normality and health are not equivalent terms. Sometimes, when a client from a sexually dysfunctional family tells me that his treatment goal is to "become normal," I jokingly respond, "Well, I have some good news and some bad news. The good news is that you are already normal. The bad news is that normality in this society is not very healthy." Actually my clients are saying that they are seeking healthy sexuality. When I ask both clients and other treatment professionals to define healthy sexuality, many of them begin to list types of behavior. This method is too simplistic an assessment, omitting as it does the essential characteristics of healthy sexuality.

Many people would say that vaginal intercourse between a man and a woman is an example of healthy sex. In fact, not enough information about the situation is given to judge its health. Are both partners in the act willing, or is one person forcing the other? If violence or threats of violence are involved, then we are discussing sexual assault; most of us would not endorse that as healthy. Rather than merely listing types of sexual behavior, it is more useful to apply some principles to a sexual situation.

Criteria of Healthy Sexuality

- Does the behavior agree with the person's values?
- Is it safe?
- Is it respectful of self and others?
- Is it honest?
- Is it spontaneous and playful?
- Does it increase intimacy?
- Are both partners free to choose?

Compatibility with Values

Part of self-respect is matching behavior to values. A value is an expression of what one believes is worthwhile. Some people from sexually dysfunctional families erroneously believe that their acting in a way others condemn means that they lack a value system. One way to assess your values is to remember a time when you felt guilty. If you have ever felt guilty, then you have a value system. Guilt results from doing something you think is wrong, violating one of your values. It is important to remember that values are very personal. Disagreement among people about a belief does not imply that someone has to be wrong. People from dysfunctional families commonly confuse guilt and shame. The focus is on the behavior, not the person. Shame comes from the belief that you are a bad or unworthy person. The focus is on your personhood, not merely on what you did.

Safety

One level of safety concerns physical health. Sexual behavior that exposes you to serious diseases or to the possibility of violence is clearly dangerous. Another sort of safety involves avoiding sexual behavior that can lead to loss of employment or being arrested. Examples include being sexual at work or in public places and violating professional ethical standards that forbid sexual contact between physicians or therapists and their patients. Using birth control is still another kind of precaution. If your sexual behavior might lead to an unwanted pregnancy, then sex is not safe for you. If you are not interested in conceiving and caring for a child, then it is best for you to involve yourself only in sexual activities with a very low risk of pregnancy. You can have this assurance only if you use birth control or abstain from vaginal intercourse.

Respect

Respect is concern, consideration, or courteous regard. Sounds nice, doesn't it? Respect begins with yourself. If your sexual behavior is self-respecting, then you are showing consideration toward your self.

A respectful sex partner notices how you feel and cares about your preferences. Such a person does not degrade another person's sexuality, body, or personhood. For example, the persistent use of sexual terms that a partner finds insulting is disrespectful. A person who continues to pressure a partner for sexual behaviors he says he does not enjoy is oblivious to his needs. Anyone who participates in sexual acts that frighten or offend him is not respecting himself.

Honesty

Part of respect is honesty. When you say yes to sex, you ought to mean it. When you say you like something, your statement ought to be true. When you say no to sex, you ought to mean "No" and not "Try to talk me into it." Say "I love you" only when you actually do love someone. A sexual relationship can be safe only in conditions of trust, which can exist only in honest relationships. How can you trust someone if either of you lies to the other?

Spontaneity and Playfulness

Spontaneous people express their feelings in a natural way, free of contrivance and constraint. Spontaneity is the opposite of compulsion. There is in compulsive behavior a sense of being driven, required, or even forced to act in some preconceived fashion. In fact, a person can take part in a compulsive act and not experience any joy or satisfaction except relief from the compulsive urge.

The goal of play is fun. Playfulness is flexible, not rigid. When something stops being fun, it is time to do something else that *is* fun. Being playful means not worrying about performing "properly." Think of someone you know who is a "bad sport," for example. Probably a person comes to mind who takes the game too seriously, who can't seem to let go and relax and is always worried about doing everything right. A bad sport ignores you when you say, "Hey, take it easy—it's only a game." She's not the kind of person that you want on your team if you're trying to have fun. Neither is she the kind of person you want in your bed if you want to enjoy being sexual. Many people from sexually dysfunctional families are very surprised, even shocked, when I use the words *playful* and *sex* in the same sentence. They have always thought of sex as something very serious. The thought of laughing during sex is a radical idea to them.

Increased Emotional Intimacy

There are numerous types of intimacy, the sharing of some aspect of your self with another person for whom you have concern. Sexual intimacy is sharing your sexual self. Emotional intimacy is sharing your emotional self. People from sexually dysfunctional families frequently believe that sexual behavior automatically leads to emotional intimacy. This belief leads them to be sexual with another person before any emotional or intellectual relationship has been formed. The physical sensations of the sexual contact may be pleasant, but they do not ensure that emotional intimacy will develop. In fact, many people report that sexual contact without an emotional connection results in greater alienation than they felt before they were sexual.

Freedom of Choice

The final characteristic of healthy sexual behavior is freedom of choice for both partners. Each has the ability to say no and the assurance that any such decision will be respected. Force or coercion is obviously not respectful or emotionally safe, and it may even be physically unsafe. A more subtle instance of coercion is the threat of abandonment used to compel undesired sexual activity. These threats may be overt, such as the statement, "If you don't have sex with me now, I'll go out and find somebody who will." Threats also may be more covert—unspoken but clearly understood. A man in a relationship with a woman might make sexual overtures that she declines. If he then starts talking about how attractive a mutual acquaintance is or suggests that it is time for the couple to start seeing other people, he is using veiled threats to control his partner.

Anyone who is compulsive about sex also lacks true freedom to choose. Such a person cannot comfortably say no to sexual urges. The key word here is *comfortably*. He may be unable to resist taking part in a behavior that makes him feel miserable. He may try to set limits and make promises to himself or others, including God, and nevertheless act unwillingly, despite his best intentions.

Judging the Health of Sexual Behavior

The seven factors presented above may be used to determine whether various types of behavior are healthy. A simple example is rape. Clearly, sexual assault is not an expression of healthy sexuality. Although the act may conform to the rapist's values, it violates the principles of safety, is not respectful, is not playful, does not increase emotional intimacy, and certainly does not involve freedom of choice for the victim.

Here is a more difficult question: Is masturbation healthy sexual behavior? Look back at the criteria and decide for yourself. The answer I come to is yes and no, depending on the circumstances. Two examples illustrate the difference.

Gene masturbates at home in a room where nobody can witness him. He touches himself in a pleasing way when he is in a pleasant mood. He believes that masturbation is an acceptable sexual expression. In fact, he says it is a case of his having sex with someone he loves. He is responsible and takes care of his needs before he masturbates. He does not restrict himself to any kind of routine. He takes his time and pays attention to his body's responses. Afterward, he enjoys a sense of well-being and is comfortable with others when he leaves his house.

Gene appears to be expressing healthy sexuality. His masturbation is safe. He does not injure himself, nor does he risk legal difficulties by being seen by others and charged with indecent exposure. Masturbation fits into his values. It does not interfere with other aspects of his life. He is spontaneous and playful. His masturbation does not lead to guilt or shame; he does not avoid other people after he has masturbated. He is free to take part in the behavior or refrain, as he chooses.

In contrast, Mary masturbates when she is angry, lonely, afraid, or ashamed. She often promises herself that she will masturbate only once a day, yet she finds herself doing it several times. She masturbates while driving her automobile and at work, behind her closed door when she is having a bad day. She has done it so frequently and with such force that she has injured herself. She cannot resist the urge to masturbate, which preoccupies her until she finds a way to do it. Sometimes she just wants "to get it over with" so she can get back to the rest of her life. Afterward she calls herself a "pervert" and other names. She believes that masturbation is wrong and that she will be punished for it. Because she thinks that others are aware of her behavior, she avoids people if she has masturbated recently.

In Mary you see a very different picture from Gene. She is endangering herself and others when she masturbates while dri-

<parm}

ving. Not only is this obliviousness disrespectful of herself and others, but it actually is life-threatening. She is coerced by her compulsion to be sexual in a way that violates her own values. Therefore she lacks a sense of freedom. Her behavior prevents emotional closeness to herself and others. She is caught up in an unhealthy sexual pattern.

At this point, you may find it helpful to consider your own sexual behavior. Using the criteria you just read about, take some time to respond to the following questions about your masturbation. Answer honestly. Do not write what you think you *should* believe; write what you actually believe at this time. One way to measure what you believe is to notice what your emotions and physical sensations tell you as you write. Do you feel glad? Afraid? Guilty? Ashamed? Does your gut get tight? Does your face blush?

What, if any, type of masturbation is within your value system?

_____

Do you masturbate in a way that is safe?

_____

Is the way you masturbate respectful to yourself and others? Explain.

_____

_____

How honest with yourself are you about your masturbation? Explain.

_____

_____

When you masturbate, is it spontaneous and playful? Explain.

_____

_____

Prior to and during your masturbation, are you aware of your emotions? What are they?

_____

_____

How do you feel after you masturbate?

_____

_____

_____

How free are you to say no to yourself about masturbation? Cite examples.

_____

_____

_____

How free are you to say yes to yourself about masturbation? Cite examples.

_____

_____

_____

What did you learn about your behavior and yourself by answering these questions?

_____

_____

_____

_____

_____

_____

_____

Now think of your sexual behavior with another person and respond to the following questions. It may be helpful to think about a particular person or situation when answering.

What types of sexual behaviors are compatible with your values?

_____

_____

_____

How safe is your sexual behavior? (Consider risk of disease, physical safety, legal difficulties, damage to reputation and job, and possible loss of important relationships.)

_____

_____

_____

Is the way you are sexual respectful to yourself and your partner? Explain.

_____

_____

_____

_____

_____

_____

_____

Are you honest with yourself and your partner in sexual matters (use of birth control, any other partners, your preferences about various activities, your desire to be sexual or not)?

_____

_____

When you are sexual, are you spontaneous and playful? Explain.

_____

_____

_____

_____

_____

_____

_____

Prior to and during sexual activities, are you aware of your emotions? Explain.

_____

_____

_____

How do you feel after you are sexual?

_____

_____

_____

How free are you to say no comfortably to sexual contact? Cite examples.

_____

_____

_____

_____

How free are you to say yes comfortably to sexual contact? Cite examples.

_____

_____

_____

_____

What did you learn about your sexual behavior and yourself by answering these questions?

_____

_____

_____

_____

_____

_____

_____

_____

What did you learn about your partner(s) by answering these questions?

_____

_____

_____

_____

_____

_____

_____

_____

A reason people feel guilty when they act in healthy sexual ways is that this behavior violates dysfunctional family rules. If you were taught, overtly or covertly, that sex is dirty, disgusting, or naughty, then it follows that you should not enjoy it. When you break the family rule and enjoy your sexuality, you may feel guilty, as if you were doing something bad, even though you are behaving in a healthy way. Guilt or fear is usually a sign that the person who feels it is doing something bad or dangerous and ought to stop. That common sense does not always hold up, however, particularly early in recovery.

Here is the last paradox of Characteristic Eight. *Sometimes* in recovery, when people feel guilt and fear about something they are doing, they ought to do more of it until they don't feel guilty or afraid anymore. I heard a woman say that she never talked during sex; since she was silent, she could never tell her partner what she enjoyed and what she wanted.

I asked her whether she thought it appropriate to talk during a meal, expressing pleasure at the enjoyment of eating and asking others at the table to pass her the foods she wanted. Of course she thought talking at meals was all right, but she balked at the idea of talking while being sexual with someone. She was caught up in the idea that sex is "dirty, disgusting, or naughty" and thus should not be talked about. Eventually she began to talk with her partner and her guilt and fear stopped. She had replaced her old, dysfunctional rule (since sex is bad, it is bad to talk during sex) with a new, healthy rule (I can ask for what I want and express my feelings, whatever I am doing).

Notice that I said it is *sometimes* a good idea to act, even though you feel afraid and guilty. These emotions do serve as the "instinct" or sixth sense that tells you when your behavior is self-defeating. How do you know whether you are changing a bad habit or ignoring a legitimate warning? Sometimes you don't know. For that reason, women and men benefit from talking things over with other recovering people. The exchange of information eases decision making.

This section has focused on the emotions related to healthy sexuality. As you respond to the following questions, observe your feelings when you read the question and while you write your answer.

Write a healthy sexual fantasy. Remember the seven criteria for healthy sex found on page 53. Pay attention to your fear or shame as you write.

What are you thinking that causes you to feel afraid or ashamed?

How are these messages related to your experience in a sexually dysfunctional family?

_____

_____

_____

_____

_____

_____

_____

_____

With what positive messages can you replace these negative messages?

_____

_____

_____

_____

_____

_____

_____

_____

How can you comfort yourself and obtain comfort and reassurance from your partner when you are being sexual?

Characteristic Nine: Misuse of Sex

As adults, many of us misidentified the roles of sex in relationships, attempting to use sex to avoid abandonment, control others, or fill our emptiness.

People use sex for many purposes, some better than others. Some people have sex to make babies, some to make money. Sex is fun or it is one way to express the affection in a relationship. One person has sex out of duty, while another is sexual out of fear and shame.

What are the reasons you have sex?

_____

_____

_____

_____

_____

_____

_____

_____

_____

_____

_____

_____

_____

In order to determine whether and how Characteristic Nine applies to your life, decide whether you agree with the following statements:

- When someone has sex with me, it means the person accepts me as a worthwhile person.
- Sex can make someone care about me.
- Sex will prevent someone who wants to go from leaving me.
- If I have enough sex, or the right type of sex, then I will like myself.

What did you learn about yourself from your responses?

_____

_____

_____

_____

_____

_____

_____

Many people from sexually dysfunctional families believe the above statements, even though they are irrational. If you don't like yourself, for example, how many times a day would you have to masturbate before you would like yourself? How many sex partners would you require before you liked yourself? As you can see from trying to answer these questions, they are based in irrational beliefs.

In my clinical experience, many of the people who come from dysfunctional families fear abandonment because as children they were neglected or emotionally abandoned by their parents. The dysfunctions (notice it is plural, since there may be more than one type of dysfunction) were so severe in some cases that the adults in the family were preoccupied with coping with their problems and had little or no time and energy left to devote to their children. Over half (54 percent) of the members of ACSD reported that, when they were young, their parents or guardians had problems related to chemical abuse. Not only was there sexual dysfunction in the family, but there were additional problems related to alcoholism and other drug addictions. An addiction of any kind prevents a person from being emotionally available. Intimacy dysfunction contributes to sexual dysfunction, which leads to all of the characteristics identified by the members of ACSD.

People from sexually dysfunctional families deal with a fear of abandonment by leaving their partners before their partners can leave them. What results is a trail of hurriedly ended relationships and a great deal of pain. This technique of coping with fear leads people to terminate a relationship prematurely at the first sign of conflict. I say prematurely because, if the level of intimacy in a relationship is to increase, disagreements and tension must arise. If you leave every time there is a potential for conflict, you miss the opportunity for the relationship to develop into something deep and meaningful. (Of course, you can go to the other extreme and stay in a relationship that has never been intimate and has no chance of becoming intimate, which is just as self-defeating.)

Characteristic Ten: Confusion of Sex with Emotions

As adults, many of us confused sex with emotional intimacy.

Characteristic Ten is closely associated with Characteristic Seven, which concerns difficulty with intimacy. Some people use the word *intimacy* as a code word for sexual activity. Often when I ask a client how intimate his relationships are, I hear, "Well, we have intimacy about twice a week; if the kids are away, then we do it more often." Rather than thinking of intimacy only as a sexual term, try viewing it as a word that describes communication or familiarity.

Intimacy, in part, means disclosure or expression of your person. The word comes from a Latin word meaning *innermost*.

When you share your body with a willing partner in a hug, an arm on the shoulder, or the touch of hands, you are being *physically intimate*. When you disclose your personal thoughts, such as what you think of yourself, you are being *mentally intimate*. When you express your emotions in the presence of an empathic person who wants to hear them, you experience *emotional intimacy*. *Sexual intimacy* occurs when you have willing sexual contact with another person. *Spiritual intimacy* is the experience of being connected with a higher power, either in solitude or in the presence of others.

People misunderstand this concept all the time. They have sex with kids and call that abuse intimacy. They intrude in others' lives and call those broken boundaries intimacy. Willingness is involved in true intimacy. It is an interchange that enriches the lives of all the parties to it. It is not a burden for anyone but improves a relationship and strengthens the bonds between people. The intensity increases when you combine several types of intimacy at once. For example, telling someone that you are glad you know him (emotional intimacy) is a more intense experience if you are hugging (physical intimacy) than if you are standing across the room. A fully clothed hug is less physically intimate than a wrestling match in a gym, but the element of emotional intimacy intensifies the meaning of the first exchange.

Since people from sexually dysfunctional families tend to confuse sex and emotional intimacy, they sometimes leave groups or end friendships when they start to grow close. They fear that the next step after any type of intimacy will be sex. Another common problem is jealousy. They assume that, if a partner or spouse is friendly or emotionally close to another person, there must be some sexual contact or at least a desire to be sexual.

Some people from sexually dysfunctional families, particularly those that overvalued sex, sexualize their emotions. Each time a person experiences an emotion, he believes it is a signal to be sexual, and consequently he misinterprets many body sensations and emotional states as "horniness." For example, someone who is frightened and has shallow breathing, sweaty palms, and a rapid heartbeat may misread these signs and call them sexual excitement. The problem with confusing fear and sexual excitement is the failure to "listen" to the signal of danger that ought to be avoided.

Another example is the person who confuses shame and sexual arousal. He feels ashamed and is sexual with someone. The sexual stimulation may be pleasant; since he has not dealt with his shame, however, he still feels ashamed after the sexual contact, perhaps even more than he felt initially.

What prevents the dispersal of shame? People who feel shame experience themselves as unworthy, not-good-enough, bad persons. Wouldn't you think that having sex with someone would prove that you are worthwhile, good enough, and desirable? That proof is often what the person who initiates the sexual contact is looking for, but this means of reassuring himself does not work. The shame he was experiencing before and during sex was secret, and shame kept secret is shame that grows. In order to reduce the shame, he would have had to disclose it to his partner.

"Oh, no!" you say. "Not that! What an order! I can't go through with it. The last thing I want to do when I am ashamed is to let somebody know how I feel." But that self-revelation is how shame is healed. During the actual experience of feeling ashamed, you express it to another person who still accepts you despite your view of yourself at the moment. Shame kept secret breeds more shame. Shame disclosed in the context of a supportive relationship is shame reduced.

One of the possible outcomes of growing up in a sexually dysfunctional family is sexual compulsiveness. Sexualized emotion can lead to compulsive sexual behavior. Thirty-seven percent of the members of ACSD describe themselves as sexually addicted. Another outcome of being raised in a sexually dysfunctional setting is the likelihood of forming adult relationships with people who are sexually compulsive. Over half of the members of ACSD (54 percent) reported that at least one or more of their past partners or spouses had been compulsive about sex. Approximately 4 percent of the members stated that their current partner was sexually compulsive. Sex addicts and their partners share beliefs about the world, some of which are expressed in the Characteristics of ACSD.

CHAPTER FOUR

Recovery

Perhaps the most destructive consequence of living as a child in a sexually dysfunctional family is the development of a shame-based identity. Children who have been neglected, abused, or repeatedly put in no-win situations develop a self-image founded in the misconception that they are worthless, do not deserve to be treated respectfully, and cannot do anything right. Even after they become adults and leave the shame-inducing environment of the family home, they still remain ashamed. In their minds, they continue to call themselves names and perpetuate the shaming dynamic learned in childhood.

When they make mistakes, they think, You should have known better! Why can't you do anything right? You'll never amount to anything!

Even when they are successful, they never give themselves a break. Who do I think I am to make such a big deal out of this? they ask themselves. It was no big deal. I should have done it sooner. Lots of other people could have done it too.

When others compliment such a person, the shaming silently continues: Yeah, you say you like me, but, if you only knew the *real* me, you wouldn't like me at all.

A shame-based identity results from neglectful or abusive relationships. Attempts to heal shame in isolation are therefore ineffective. A wound caused by a relationship with another person requires a relationship to heal it. For that reason, I am not afraid that my role as a psychotherapist can be filled by a machine, not even by one that could ask the right questions and give the correct responses. Shame is induced person to person, and the healing of shame requires safe, nurturing person-to-person interaction.

A shame-based identity is distorted. The correction of mis-perceptions requires interaction with another person. I call this exchange a "reality check." A person who is telling himself that he is worthless and unlovable needs to determine whether his view is accurate; perhaps he is merely suffering shame. He can distinguish only by checking out his perceptions with reliable others. If he keeps his thoughts and emotions to himself, he never gets the opportunity to challenge their accuracy.

Suppose that a woman accidentally knocks over her cof-fee cup at a friend's house. He helps her clean up the spill, and they return to their conversation. All the while, however, she is worrying, He thinks I am a clumsy slob. He wishes I would just leave. He'll never want me to come to his home again.

If she keeps her shame to herself, she never will know whether her interpretations are correct. She cannot focus com-pletely on the current conversation because she is too busy looking for clues that her assumptions are accurate. In addition, during future get-togethers with her friend, she may assume that he views her as a clumsy slob.

Suppose, however, that she decides to risk saying to her friend, "I'm sorry I'm not all here at the moment. I was worrying that you might not like me anymore because I made a mess."

If her friend is indeed a friend, he will assure her that he accepts her and hopes to continue being friends. "No problem," he might say. "I know it was just an accident. I'm not about to let something little like that come between us."

Since shame is induced by abusive or neglectful relation-ships with others, recovery from shame requires nurturing, supportive relationships with others. A solo plan will not get you very far; you need to interact with others.

How Does a Twelve Step Program Help?

A mutual-help group assists in several ways. To begin with, attending a group, such as Adult Chidren of Sexual Dysfunction, supplies the problem with a name, and with a focus. Rather than think that you're crazy, stupid, or bad, you realize that many of your present problems are the logical outcome of your childhood family's attitudes. Membership in a group also gives you the emotional support of others. As I wrote earlier, shame is healed in supportive relationships. A group can provide such interactions with people who truly understand your problems and struggles. Many members of mutual-help groups say that the group members become a surrogate family. Groups that recommend sponsorship provide a relationship between established members and new ones that is similar to that between healthy parents and children. The sponsor is available to help the newer member to grow and mature in recovery.

A group based on the Twelve Steps also offers a time-proven framework for working on problems. Fellowships that do not use the process that originated in Alcoholics Anonymous frequently are able to identify problems but lack a structure for making stable changes. The Twelve Steps can best be understood as a shame-reduction program. The first three Steps develop a relationship with a loving Higher Power. Then the Fourth through Seventh Steps help heal the member's shame-based sense of self. The Eighth and Ninth help mend damaged relationships with others. Finally, the Tenth through the Twelfth provide a maintenance program to keep shame at a minimum.

The Twelve Steps of Alcoholics Anonymous

1. We admitted we were powerless over alcohol—that our lives had become unmanageable.

2. Came to believe that a Power greater than ourselves could restore us to sanity.

3. Made a decision to turn our will and our lives over to the care of God, as we understood Him.

4. Made a searching and fearless moral inventory of ourselves.

5. Admitted to God, to ourselves, and to another human being the exact nature of our wrongs.

6. Were entirely ready to have God remove all these defects of character.

7. Humbly asked Him to remove our shortcomings.

8. Made a list of all persons we had harmed and became willing to make amends to them all.

9. Made direct amends to such people wherever possible, except when to do so would injure them or others.

10. Continued to take personal inventory and when we were wrong, promptly admitted it.

11. Sought through prayer and meditation to improve our conscious contact with God, as we understood Him, praying only for knowledge of His will for us and the power to carry that out.

12. Having had a spiritual awakening as the result of these Steps, we tried to carry this message to other alcoholics and to practice these principles in all our affairs.

The Twelve Steps Adapted for Adult Children of Sexual Dysfunction

1. We admitted that we were powerless over sexual dysfunction—that our lives had become unmanageable.

2. Came to believe that a Power greater than ourselves could restore us to sanity.

3. Made a decision to turn our will and our lives over to the care of God, as we understood God.

4. Made a searching and fearless moral inventory of ourselves.

5. Admitted to God, to ourselves, and to another human being the exact nature of our wrongs.

6. Were entirely ready to have God remove all these defects of character.

7. Humbly asked God to remove our shortcomings.

8. Made a list of all persons we had harmed, and became willing to make amends to them all.

9. Made direct amends to such people wherever possible, except when to do so would injure them or others.

10. Continued to take personal inventory and when we were wrong, promptly admitted it.

11. Sought through prayer and meditation to improve our conscious contact with God, as we understood God, praying only for knowledge of God's will for us and the power to carry that out.

12. Having had a spiritual awakening as the result of these Steps, we tried to carry this message to others and to practice these principles in all our affairs.

The experience of members in ACSD has led them to describe what others can expect to gain from applying the Twelve Steps to daily living:

The Promises of Adult Children of Sexual Dysfunction

Our experiences have shown that if you honestly apply this program to your life you will come to know a freedom, self-acceptance, and joy unknown to you before. Irrational fears will be eliminated. You will take responsibility for the direction of your life, understanding the past and looking to the future with hope. Intimacy and joyous sexuality will be yours. You will find yourself a part of a community of people who share a commitment to a life filled with healing spirituality, healthy sexuality, and emotional well-being. You will know serenity.

Why Not Recover in Another Twelve Step Group?

Although some newcomers to ACSD have never attended another Twelve Step group, many members have tried other recovery programs (see the Appendix). These people were less successful in their efforts to heal from the effects of living in a sexually dysfunctional family until they joined the group that focuses specifically on this issue. Most other programs are not designed to discuss in detail the pain of life in a sexually dysfunctional family. Many people say that, when they tried to talk about their sexual issues in other groups, they were met with resistance.

Many of the problems dealt with in Twelve Step organizations are related to sex and relationship issues. Addiction of any kind prevents a parent's emotional availability to children. If the parent is not available to bond with a child and teach intimacy, the child will become an adult who lacks the ability to form satisfying relationships, which, in turn, leads to sexual problems.

Once people address their compulsive sexual behavior, overeating, drug misuse, or other consequences of a dysfunctional family, the attitudes described in the Characteristics of ACSD still remain. The need for a group of other adult children becomes more apparent.

All members of ACSD can relate to the others' experiences. Most people who attend Twelve Step groups come in with a great deal of shame. It is therefore important that, when you tell your history to others, you choose people who understand what you went through and how it affected you. It is not helpful to tell your personal story to someone who responds, "How weird. I've never heard anything like that before. Why don't you stop doing those things? You should know better." When you are vulnerable, you need others who understand and accept you. They needn't have had exactly the same experiences. Similar backgrounds can give them empathy and knowledge of what you have felt.

Nearly everything you have read to this point has focused on the problems caused by being raised in a sexually dysfunctional family. Many of these problems you already were familiar with—you were living with them every day. The remainder of the book presents principles that will help you change the attitudes and behaviors that prevent your living a full life. Here again you will gain more understanding of yourself if you go slowly and actually write out a response to each question. Although it will be a painful process, it also will be rewarding.

A Twelve Step Guide

The pain of living with the powerlessness and unmanageability related to having been reared by sexually dysfunctional people is what drives people to seek recovery. The Twelve Step program is often described as a simple program for complex people: the ACSD Characteristics describe the problem, the ACSD Promises (see page 78) describe the outcome of recovery, and the Twelve Steps (see page 77) describe the recovery process.

The First Step is the beginning of any program based on the AA Twelve Steps. Properly done, it paves the way for the remaining eleven Steps and a complete recovery. Once you have responded to all of the questions related to this Step, set up a time to meet someone you trust to discuss what you have written. This conversation will help you to gain further insights and to reduce the shame, sadness, and loneliness you may feel as a result of exploring your past.

Step One

We admitted we were powerless over sexual dysfunction—
that our lives had become unmanageable.

Powerlessness

Probably the least appealing word in the Twelve Steps is *power-lessness*. Who wants to acknowledge that he or she is without power, disabled, incapacitated? Unattractive as the concept is, however, powerlessness does describe in a single word what being a child in a sexually dysfunctional family is all about. Powerlessness can be understood in two ways. First, the concept pertains to the inability to prevent certain things from occurring. Children are powerless in this way, unable to avoid being sexually abused, shamed, hit, made fun of, ignored, or called names. The idea of powerlessness also refers to the inability to bring about desired results. Children cannot make their parents spend time with them, provide nourishing touch, or supply essential information about sex.

Many people avoid seeing their childhood powerlessness by focusing on the ways they are powerful as adults. They point to the power in their careers, their status, or title. Some people believe that their ability to intimidate, coerce, or assault others is "proof" that they are not powerless.

In order to determine whether you were powerless over sexual dysfunction as a child, ask yourself the following questions. Remember when responding to pay attention to what your emotions and physical sensations tell you. Do you feel glad? Afraid? Guilty? Ashamed? Does your gut get tight? Does your face blush?

As a child, were you easily able to obtain appropriate, accurate, and useful information about sex?

☐ Yes ☐ No

As a child, were you free to be accepting of your body, gender, and sexuality?

☐ Yes   ☐ No

As a child, were you easily able to view sex in a balanced way?

☐ Yes   ☐ No

As a child, could you prevent others from making disrespectful remarks or exhibiting disrespectful behaviors about gender and sexuality?

☐ Yes   ☐ No

As a child, could you obtain nourishing touch?

☐ Yes   ☐ No

What did you learn by responding to these questions?

_____

_____

_____

_____

_____

_____

_____

_____

Unmanageability

If *powerlessness* is the least appealing word in the Twelve Steps, *unmanageability* is nearly as unpleasant. Nevertheless, it is the out-of-control everyday life that makes recovery groups necessary. If being powerless as a child didn't lead to unmanageable adulthoods, all you would have to do to recover is grow older. Unfortunately, time alone does not heal all wounds. Powerlessness in childhood leads to a disrupted adulthood, which creates the need for recovery programs.

The following questions focus on various elements of Step One, which are indicated by boldface type.

WE ADMITTED THAT WE WERE POWERLESS OVER SEXUAL DYSFUNCTION—THAT OUR LIVES HAD BECOME UNMANAGEABLE.

Shame is the result of abusive or neglectful relationships. It is the result of some*one*, not some*thing*, harming you. Abuse is not some effect that *happens to you*, it is an act *done to you*. It is interpersonal. It happens in a relationship with another person. Therefore, the healing of shame requires respectful interactions with others. The first word of the First Step acknowledges the interpersonal nature of recovery. The word *we* points out that recovery is something done with others, not alone, in isolation. The first task of the First Step is to consider how you have remained distant from others. Then you can begin to think about what you can do to change this self-defeating pattern.

As an adult, in what ways have you behaved that have kept you distant from others?

_____

_____

_____

_____

_____

_____

_____

_____

What can you do to allow others to help you overcome the effects of living in a sexually dysfunctional family?

_____

_____

_____

_____

_____

_____

_____

_____

How has being the adult child of a sexually dysfunctional family kept you isolated?

_____

_____

_____

_____

_____

_____

_____

List the names of three people you believe you can trust to help you overcome the effects of having lived in a sexually dysfunctional family.

_____

Now write how you will invite them to help you and a date by which you will do so.

_____

_____

_____

_____

_____

_____

_____

WE ADMITTED THAT WE WERE **POWERLESS OVER SEXUAL DYSFUNCTION**—THAT OUR LIVES HAD BECOME UNMANAGEABLE.

In childhood, who told you about sex? What were you told *verbally* about sexuality?

_____

_____

_____

_____

_____

_____

_____

What did you learn about sexuality by watching the adults in your family?

_____

_____

_____

_____

_____

_____

What was the quality of your childhood information about sexuality? Was it inappropriate? If so, how?

_____

_____

_____

_____

_____

Was it inaccurate? What was inaccurate about it?

_____

_____

_____

_____

_____

Was it useful? If not, explain.

_____

_____

_____

_____

_____

In your adolescence, who told you about sex? What were you told *verbally* about sexuality?

_____

_____

_____

_____

_____

_____

_____

_____

What did you learn as a teenager about sexuality by watching the adults in your family?

_____

_____

_____

_____

_____

_____

_____

_____

What was the quality of the information you learned about sexuality as a teenager? Was it inappropriate? If so, how?

_____

_____

_____

_____

Was it inaccurate? What was inaccurate about it?

_____

_____

_____

_____

Was it useful? If not, explain.

_____

_____

_____

What will you do to obtain appropriate, accurate, and useful information about sexuality (such as take a class in human sexuality, get a book about sexuality from the library, or talk with a trusted person)?

_____

_____

_____

How have you experienced shame or confusion about your body?

_____

_____

_____

Others' bodies?

_____

_____

_____

Your gender?

_____

_____

_____

The other gender?

_____

_____

_____

Sexuality?

_____

_____

Of the three types of sexually dysfunctional family styles described in this book (overvaluing sex, negative toward sex, and sexually shut down), which did your family most resemble? (Remember that you determine what "family" means to you. Family consists of the people you learned from, whether or not they were related to you.)

_____

_____

_____

_____

_____

_____

_____

How did this family style affect you?

_____

_____

_____

_____

_____

_____

_____

In your family, was sex viewed as all-important? If so, how did you learn this?

_____

_____

_____

_____

_____

_____

_____

_____

In your family, was sex viewed as dirty, disgusting, or naughty? If so, how did you learn this?

_____

_____

_____

_____

_____

_____

_____

_____

List examples of disrespectful behaviors or remarks about gender and sexuality that you witnessed in your family.

_____

_____

_____

_____

_____

_____

_____

_____

What did you learn from witnessing these behaviors or remarks?

_____

_____

_____

_____

_____

_____

_____

_____

_____

What kind of touch did you experience in your family?

_____

_____

_____

_____

_____

_____

_____

What can you do to obtain safe, nourishing touch from *yourself*?

_____

_____

_____

_____

_____

_____

_____

_____

What can you do to obtain safe, nourishing touch from *others?* (For example, you may decide to pay a massage therapist to touch you in a safe environment, pet an animal, or hold a group member's hand during the closing ritual at a Twelve Step meeting.)

_____

_____

_____

_____

_____

_____

_____

_____

How will you recognize safe, nurturing touch when you obtain it?

_____

_____

_____

_____

_____

_____

_____

_____

WE ADMITTED THAT WE WERE POWERLESS OVER SEXUAL DYSFUNCTION—**THAT OUR LIVES HAD BECOME UNMAN-AGEABLE.**

As an adult, faced with sexual situations, how have you experienced confusion?

_____

_____

_____

_____

_____

_____

_____

Discomfort?

_____

_____

_____

_____

_____

_____

_____

Terror?

_____

_____

_____

_____

_____

_____

_____

As an adult, how have you experienced difficulties in establishing intimate relationships with others?

_____

_____

_____

_____

_____

_____

_____

_____

When you act in a healthy sexual way, how do you experience fear?

_____

_____

_____

_____

_____

_____

_____

_____

Shame?

_____

_____

_____

_____

_____

_____

_____

_____

_____

How have you attempted to use sex to avoid abandonment?

_____

_____

_____

_____

_____

_____

_____

_____

What was the result of this behavior?

_____

_____

_____

_____

_____

_____

_____

_____

How have you attempted to use sex to control others?

_____

_____

_____

_____

_____

_____

_____

_____

_____

What was the result of this behavior?

_____

_____

_____

_____

_____

_____

_____

_____

How have you attempted to use sex to fill your emptiness?

_____
_____
_____
_____
_____
_____
_____
_____

What was the result of this behavior?

_____
_____
_____
_____
_____
_____
_____

How have you confused sex with emotional intimacy?

_____

_____

_____

_____

_____

_____

_____

_____

What was the result of this behavior?

_____

_____

_____

_____

_____

_____

_____

Write your definition of emotional intimacy.

_____

_____

_____

_____

_____

_____

_____

_____

_____

How are emotional intimacy and sexual intimacy different?

_____

_____

_____

_____

_____

_____

_____

_____

Have you ever experienced emotional intimacy and sexual intimacy simultaneously? If so, what made this possible?

_____

_____

_____

_____

_____

_____

_____

Once you have an understanding of how you have been affected by your experience in a sexually dysfunctional family, you are ready to move toward Step Two and healing.

Step Two

Came to believe that a Power greater than ourselves could restore us to sanity.

Answering the First Step questions, you no doubt saw that, in your childhood, there was a power greater than yourself: the adults who neglected or abused you. This fact lead to the symptoms described in the first five Characteristics of ACSD. The Second Step asks you to consider the idea that, just as a power greater than yourself caused you to lead a dysfunctional life, another power can restore you to a joyful life. The Second Step is hopeful; it says you can _re_store yourself to sanity. This language points out that you were not born with the Characteristics you have been reading about. Your rightful, natural state is not dysfunctional, but sane and serene. The Second Step does not spell out what the power greater than yourself must be. You decide what you believe. You are responsible to make that determination.

The Second Step really asks a question: What do you believe can restore you to a sane life? Notice you are not merely being asked, *Do you believe* that something can help you? You also are asked, *What do you believe* can help you?

Now seems like an appropriate time to answer those very questions.

Do you believe that there is a power greater than you that can restore you to sanity?

☐ Yes   ☐ No

What is this power? Describe it.

_____

_____

_____

_____

_____

_____

_____

Step Three

Made a decision to turn our will and our lives over to the care of God, as we understood God.

Turning your will and life over to a higher power means that you agree to think and behave differently. When you work the Third Step you are thinking and acting in a manner unlike the style described in the ACSD Characteristics.

Some people become bogged down with this Step because they have been taught that God is an angry, punishing force to be feared. Others resist this Step because, on some level, when they think of a power greater than themselves, they automatically think about an abusive or neglectful parent. If you are rebellious here, return to the Second Step and work to create an image of a safe, nurturing, supportive, caring higher power. Notice the words of the Step: "care of God." Although it is difficult and frightening to decide to turn your will and life over to a dangerous God, it is much easier and comforting to trust the care of a power that has your best interests in mind.

It will be helpful for you now to give some thought to how you can apply the Third Step to your own life.

What are some **actions** that you can take to turn your will and life over to the care of the power you have defined (get a sponsor, attend Twelve Step meetings, read about recovery daily)? List the behaviors to which you will commit yourself this month as a private sign that you are working the Third Step.

Step Four

Made a searching and fearless moral inventory of ourselves.

Sometimes people ask, "How will I know when I have truly taken the Third Step seriously?" Put simply, people do know when they are following through on the remaining Steps. A Fourth Step shows that you are putting your Third Step decision into action. You begin to behave in a way that suggests belief in a power that will assist you in recovering from the past.

Step Four speaks of a moral inventory. "Moral" pertains to distinguishing between right and wrong. Everyone I know who seeks a recovery program is able to do this. In fact, it is this ability to experience guilt when they wrong someone that causes people to seek help.

The Fourth Step asks the question, Who are you, other than an adult child from a sexually dysfunctional family? In the First Step, you looked at the ways the ACSD Characteristics apply to your life. Now you examine other aspects of your character. This inventory is necessary to the completion of the remaining Steps. Many people get stuck at Step Three and never get around to working on Step Four. The main obstacle to a moral inventory is the perfectionism of adult children from any type of dysfunctional family and their habitual unkindness to themselves. When I'm speaking publicly on the topic of dysfunctional families, I often ask the audience, "How many of you have ever actually made a mistake?" Everyone raises a hand. "How many have told yourselves you are worthless and unlovable if you make a mistake?" I ask. Nearly everyone raises a hand. "How comfortable would you be turning to the person next to you, who just admitted mistakes, and saying 'You are worthless and unlovable?'" Most people report that they are very unwilling to say to their neighbors the very thing they say to themselves all day long.

Recovery means not only "Love thy neighbor as thyself," but also "Love thyself as thy neighbor." In other words, don't say or think things about yourself that you would not be willing to say to someone else you cared about. One of the signs of restoration to sanity (remember Step Two?) is beginning to treat yourself with as much respect as you treat other people.

Who are you other than an adult child from a sexually dysfunctional family? List some words to describe yourself. Explain with examples.

What personal assets do you possess to assist you in your recovery (honesty, diligence, dedication, intelligence, commitment, openness, willingness to ask for help, ability to listen to others and learn from them)? Explain with examples.

_____

_____

_____

_____

_____

_____

_____

_____

_____

Step Five

Admitted to God, to ourselves, and to another human being the exact nature of our wrongs.

To this point, using the Steps has been a process of acceptance and assessment: you found the source of your difficulties (Step One); you identified your belief in a healing power (Step Two); you chose to accept its help (Step Three); and you found out that you are more than you took credit for (Step Four). Now you are ready to put all of that work into action by talking with another person about what blocks your fulfillment and happiness.

The First Step invited you to stop keeping secrets about your family. The Fourth Step invited you to stop keeping secrets *about* yourself, *from* yourself. The Fifth Step now invites you to stop keeping secrets about yourself from God and humanity.

Once you have written your response to the Fourth Step, ask someone you trust to listen to what you have written.

The Fifth Step asks you some powerful questions:

Do you believe you can truly know yourself and still love yourself?

☐ Yes   ☐ No

Do you believe you can show your true self to God and to another human being and still be accepted?

☐ Yes   ☐ No

If your answers were no, perhaps some additional work on the previous Steps is in order, or assistance from a trained therapist, such as a psychologist, clinical social worker, or marriage and family therapist.

Step Six

Were entirely ready to have God remove all these defects of character.

While working on your Fourth Step you identified your assets and your liabilities. Some of these ways of thinking and acting you are anxious to be rid of. Even so, at the same time, you may want to hold on to some of the very patterns of thinking and behaving that are currently causing you problems. This desire, at first glance, seems less than sane. What would motivate someone to cling to attitudes and acts that lead to pain and despair? It cannot be ignorance. The First Step showed you that the ACSD Characteristics were alive and operating in your life.

The cause of the resistance is the fact that these character defects were once very useful. In other words, what is currently a defect of adult character was once the coping mechanism of a trapped child. The adult character defect, isolation and avoidance of any touch, is a remnant of childhood coping with deprivation of touch (Characteristic Five) and a defense against disrespectful behaviors or remarks (Characteristic Four). The child appropriately tried to avoid being hurt further by withdrawing from those who were responsible for the neglect or abuse. An adult can exercise choices that were not available to the child, however. The situation, the surroundings, the type of people have changed, yet the behavior persists. It no longer protects, but now adds to the problem. An obsolete coping style ought to be discarded—or in the words of the Sixth Step, removed by the God of your understanding.

Do you believe that your character defects are merely the obsolete remnants of defense mechanisms developed by a child who was trying to survive in a sexually dysfunctional family?

☐ Yes   ☐ No

If no, refer to your First Step again. If yes, then continue.

Write a list of your character defects (it may help to refer to your Fourth Step). Cite examples.

_____

_____

_____

_____

_____

_____

_____

_____

For each character defect you identified, write how it was useful to you at one time.

_____

_____

_____

_____

_____

_____

_____

For each character defect you identified, write how it has become obsolete.

_____

_____

_____

_____

_____

_____

_____

_____

How will you be as a person when these defects of character have been removed?

_____

_____

_____

_____

_____

_____

_____

_____

_____

_____

Step Seven

Humbly asked God to remove our shortcomings.

The Seventh Step gives you the opportunity, once again, to apply the Third Step to your life (Made a decision to turn our will and our lives over to the care of God, as we understood God). Working the Seventh Step, you assume that, if you are willing, you can be free of your old defects, the Characteristics.

By the time you reach the Seventh Step, you are more than halfway through the Twelve Step Program. Now is a time to take an inventory of your progress and see how working the Steps has affected your life. Write examples to answer all of these questions.

How have you gained appropriate, accurate, and useful information about sex, gender, and sexuality?

_____

_____

_____

_____

_____

_____

_____

_____

How has your shame or confusion about your body, gender, and sexuality been reduced?

_____

_____

_____

_____

_____

_____

_____

How have you come to view sex in less extreme terms, so that you no longer see it as all-important or dirty, disgusting, or naughty?

_____

_____

_____

_____

_____

_____

_____

_____

How do you resist and reject disrespectful behaviors or remarks about gender and sexuality?

_____

_____

_____

_____

_____

_____

_____

_____

How do you obtain and enjoy nourishing touch?

_____

_____

_____

_____

_____

_____

_____

_____

How have your confusion, discomfort, or terror in the face of
sexuality been reduced or eliminated?

_____

_____

_____

_____

_____

_____

_____

_____

How have you learned to establish intimate relationships with less difficulty?

_____

_____

_____

_____

_____

_____

_____

_____

How have you dealt with fear or shame so that these emotions trouble you less when you act in healthy sexual ways?

_____

_____

_____

_____

_____

_____

_____

_____

Cite some examples of your overcoming the tendency to misidentify the roles of sex in relationships, and attempting to use sex to avoid abandonment, control others, or fill emptiness.

_____

_____

_____

_____

_____

_____

_____

_____

Give some examples of your learning to distinguish sex from emotional intimacy.

_____

_____

_____

_____

_____

_____

_____

_____

Step Eight

Made a list of all persons we had harmed, and became willing to make amends to them all.

Step Eight asks you to acknowledge that your character defects (review your Fourth Step) and the effects of the ACSD Characteristics have caused you to behave in ways that have harmed others. People tend to focus on the injuries they suffered as children in a dysfunctional family (those found in the childhood Characteristics and Step One) and overlook the harm they have done others in adulthood (as found in the adulthood Characteristics). But remember that the ACSD Promises state, "if you honestly apply this program to your life," then you must "take responsibility for the direction of your life, understanding the past and looking to the future with hope." That hope will be plausible because, by working the Steps, you will assure that the Characteristics no longer rule your attitudes and behavior. Your life, therefore, will no longer be unmanageable.

Many adult children from dysfunctional families harm others, not by what they do to other people, but rather by what they do *not* do. The ACSD Characteristics prevented you from being intimate with others. This aloofness harmed them by cutting them off from someone they cared about and wanted to be close to. Naturally, you were harmed by this inability to be intimate as well.

Remember to "love thyself as thy neighbor." Be gentle with yourself as you review the effects of your past behavior. Speak to yourself as you would to somebody else whom you love and treat with respect. If your shame or guilt overwhelms you, stop and phone or visit someone. Remember, the Twelve Steps are a *we* program, not a solo plan.

Set aside some time for yourself in order to reflect on the usefulness of the Eighth Step. Then respond to the following questions.

How did your having harmful information about sex harm others? (You may have passed on harmful information about sex to your children; you may have acted in ways that hurt your sex partner.)

_____

_____

_____

_____

_____

_____

_____

Describe how your shame or confusion about your body, gender, and sexuality caused you to behave in a manner that harmed another person. (Your inability to accept pleasure from an interested sex partner may have hurt someone who loved you.)

_____

_____

_____

_____

_____

_____

_____

Whom (besides yourself) did you harm with your extreme view of sex as all-important or as dirty, disgusting, or naughty? (You may have shamed a child for masturbating or otherwise exploring his body; you may have insisted on having sex despite your partner's not feeling physically well or emotionally available.)

_____

_____

_____

_____

_____

_____

_____

Write the names of people you harmed by behaving or talking disrespectfully about gender or sexuality. Specify what you did or said that was injurious. (You may have used sexist language or told homophobic jokes.)

_____

_____

_____

_____

_____

_____

_____

Describe incidents (including people's names) when you touched others in a non-nourishing manner. (You may have been rough or violent.)

_____

_____

_____

_____

_____

_____

_____

List people you have harmed by refusing to accept their appropriate touch or by withholding appropriate touch. Whom did you harm when you experienced confusion, discomfort, or terror in the face of sexuality? (Did you blame someone for your discomfort in a sexual situation when that person was acting appropriately?)

_____

_____

_____

_____

_____

_____

_____

Whom have you harmed by your inability to establish intimate relationships? State how they were harmed by your difficulty with intimacy. (Were you in a relationship with a person who really loved you, but with whom you were unable to be intimate, so the relationship ended?)

_____

_____

_____

_____

_____

_____

_____

How has your fear or shame when you acted in healthy sexual ways harmed another? (Has it been difficult for your partner to enjoy sex because of your emotional reaction to sexual situations?)

_____

_____

_____

_____

_____

_____

_____

Whom have you harmed by attempting to use sex to avoid abandonment?

_____

_____

_____

_____

_____

_____

_____

_____

Whom have you harmed by attempting to use sex to control another?

_____

_____

_____

_____

_____

_____

_____

_____

Whom have you harmed by attempting to use sex to fill your emptiness?

_____

_____

_____

_____

_____

_____

_____

Whom have you harmed by confusing sex with emotional intimacy?

_____

_____

_____

_____

_____

_____

_____

Step Nine

Made direct amends to such people wherever possible, except when to do so would injure them or others.

The goal of the Ninth Step is self-forgiveness. After using Step Eight to inventory those you have harmed, you are ready to determine what is necessary for you to forgive yourself and let go of the past.

Return to the questions in the worksheet section of Step Eight and your list of the people you have harmed. Review each name and what you did. Decide what would be appropriate action to make amends, to improve the relationship, to forgive yourself. Then decide whether you can take this action without doing further harm. If you are unable to make direct amends without causing additional harm, then indirect amends are called for. A person who was violent toward women or homosexuals, for example, might donate some money or time to an organization that promotes the welfare of these people. In some cases, you need only take responsibility for your actions and tell the person you harmed that you regret your behavior and will do everything in your power to see that you do not perpetuate the pattern.

Step Ten

Continued to take personal inventory and when we were wrong, promptly admitted it.

One of the character defects that can be removed or diminished as a result of the first seven Steps is shame. By the time you are working on Step Ten, you will likely be aware of the differences between guilt and shame. In later recovery, when you make a mistake (and you will—notice that the Step says, "*when* we were wrong") you feel guilty instead of ashamed.

When you experience guilt, you think, Oops, I made a mistake. I wish I hadn't done it that way. I had better seek out the person I harmed and make things right again. When you made a mistake and experienced shame, you more likely thought, Oops, there it is; proof that I am unworthy and unlovable. I shouldn't have done that. Why am I such an idiot? I had better avoid everyone so that nobody will see what a piece of trash I truly am.

Just as the Eighth and Ninth Steps help you forgive yourself for past behaviors, the Tenth Step helps you forgive yourself for current inappropriate behavior. You need only monitor your actions and, when you notice something you feel guilty about, do something to forgive yourself.

Make use of the following questions each night.

Have you done anything today that was wrong? Describe what you did.

_____

_____

_____

_____

_____

_____

_____

How did it harm you or another?

_____

_____

_____

_____

_____

_____

_____

What will you do to forgive yourself?

_____

_____

_____

_____

_____

_____

_____

Step Eleven

Sought through prayer and meditation to improve our conscious contact with God, as we understood God, praying only for knowledge of God's will for us and the power to carry that out.

One of the slogans commonly heard at Twelve Step meetings is "Keep it simple." The Twelve Step program is certainly spiritual. The concept of a higher power is mentioned in six of the Steps. However, it is a very flexible, open program. There are no dogmatic requirements about what to believe or how to interact with this higher power. The only suggestions are to turn your will and your life over to the care of the God of your understanding and to pray for "knowledge of God's will" and "the power to carry it out." What does the phrase "God's will" mean? I take this meaning to be God's desire, God's wish for me.

Do you think it is God's will that you live in accordance with the ACSD Characteristics or the Promises? In other words, do you think God's will for you is a life of shame and confusion about your body, gender, and sexuality; disrespectful behaviors and remarks about gender and sexuality; confusion, discomfort, and terror in the face of sexuality; difficulty establishing intimate relationships with others; misuse of sex to avoid reality; powerlessness and unmanageability? Or do you think that God's will for you is a life of freedom, self-acceptance, joy, responsibility, hope, healing spirituality, healthy sexuality, emotional well-being, and serenity?

What do you wish for the other members of your group, family, or other loved ones? That which you desire for others is what I hope you desire for yourself as well.

Each morning ask yourself the following question and write what you become aware of after silent reflection.

What is my God's will for me today?

_____

_____

_____

_____

_____

_____

_____

Step Twelve

Having had a spiritual awakening as the result of these Steps, we tried to carry this message to others and to practice these principles in all our affairs.

The Twelfth Step contains a promise along with a condition. It states that you will have a spiritual awakening; that is the promise. The condition is that the promise comes true "as the result of these steps" and practicing "these principles in all our affairs." The Promises of ACSD also describe the spiritual awakening that is possible: "Intimacy and joyous sexuality will be yours. You will find yourself a part of a community of people who share a commitment to a life filled with healing spirituality, healthy sexuality, and emotional well-being. You will know serenity." The Promises also point out that some effort is required for these blessings to occur: "Our experiences have shown that, if you honestly *apply this program* to your life, you will come to know a freedom, self-acceptance, and joy unknown to you before. Irrational fears will be eliminated. You will *take responsibility for the direction of your life*, understanding the past and looking to the future with hope."

What does "working your Program" mean to you? Describe your recovery program. In what ways have you "come to know a freedom, self-acceptance, and joy unknown to you before"?

_____

_____

_____

_____

_____

_____

_____

In what respects have your "irrational fears been eliminated" or reduced?

_____

_____

_____

_____

_____

_____

_____

How have you "taken responsibility for the direction of your life"?

_____

_____

_____

_____

_____

_____

_____

_____

What have you come to understand about your past and the effect it has had on your present?

_____

_____

_____

_____

_____

_____

_____

How does your new perspective show that you are "looking to the future with hope?"

_____

_____

_____

_____

_____

_____

_____

_____

How have intimacy and joyous sexuality become more a part of your life?

_____

_____

_____

_____

_____

_____

_____

_____

Describe how you are "a part of a community of people who share a commitment to a life filled with healing spirituality, healthy sexuality, and emotional well-being."

_____

_____

_____

_____

_____

_____

_____

_____

Describe serenity and describe a time when you experienced it.

_____

_____

_____

_____

_____

_____

_____

_____

CHAPTER FIVE

Conclusion

Congratulations. If you have completed the workbook to this point, you have successfully applied all ten Characteristics and the Twelve Steps to your life, a challenging task indeed. You can be proud of your efforts. It takes bravery to look back at a childhood filled with pain. It takes strength to begin to change behavior patterns and attitudes that have existed for years. By completing this book, you have initiated a process that is mentioned in the ACSD Promises. By "understanding the past," you have begun to "take responsibility for the direction of your life."

As you know, family sexual dysfunction negatively affected not just your sexuality, but also every other area of your life. Fortunately, recovery has a similarly pervasive healing impact. The early stages of recovery are naturally the most difficult. You will be glad to know that your recovery will require less effort and discomfort from here on out. Eventually it will be second nature to behave in a self-respecting, healthy manner. Very likely you already have begun to see the fruits of your labor. As you continue to apply the Steps to your life, you will begin to notice every one of the Promises coming true for you. You will see that the ACSD Characteristics are worded in the past tense because eventually they will no longer apply to your daily living.

Is what I am describing too good to be true? I know it is not. I have witnessed many people's healing and growth. They had the same doubts and fears that you may suffer. They, too, had years of dysfunction to overcome. They continued to apply this simple program of recovery to their lives every day and were miraculously changed. In the same way, you will be transformed when you carry on what you have started here.

I wrote this book in an effort to pass on to you what I have learned from years of being a part of the recovery movement. I sincerely hope it has contributed to your growth and well-being. Know that, although we may never meet, I wish you a long life filled with all the riches that recovery offers.

Appendix

Notes on a Survey of ACSD Membership

In March 1990, I distributed a questionnaire to the members of Adult Children of Sexually Dysfunctional Families in Minneapolis. At that time, the organization had been in existence for only twenty-six months; and all of the groups were located there. Twenty-four members responded, half of each gender. Their ages ranged from twenty-one to forty-seven years, with an average of thirty-six. They had been attending ACSD meetings for various lengths of time: 25 percent, less than three months; 8 percent, between three and six months; 25 percent, between seven and eleven months. Twenty-one percent had been coming between one and two years. The final 21 percent had been members for two or more years.

Response to ACSD Characteristics

ACSD Members were asked to respond to the Characteristics with one of the following replies: definitely applies to me; applies to me somewhat; or does not apply to me at all.

1. Many of us were given harmful information about sex instead of appropriate, accurate, or useful information about sex.

   Definitely applies 79%   Applies somewhat 20%

2. Many of us experienced shame or confusion about our bodies, our gender, and our sexuality.

   Definitely applies 96%   Applies somewhat 4%

3. Many of us grew up in families in which sex tended to be viewed in extremes. Sex was all-important and/or sex was dirty, disgusting, or naughty.

   Definitely applies 70%   Applies somewhat 20%

4. Many of us grew up in families in which disrespectful behaviors or remarks about gender and sexuality were common.

   Definitely applies 70%   Applies somewhat 16%

5. Many of us grew up in families in which there was a lack of nourishing touch.

   Definitely applies 83%   Applies somewhat 16%

6. As adults, many of us experienced confusion, discomfort, or terror in the face of sexuality.

   Definitely applies 87%   Applies somewhat 8%

7. As adults, many of us experienced difficulties in establishing intimate relationships.

   Definitely applies 100%

8. As adults, many of us experienced fear or shame when we acted in healthy sexual ways.

   Definitely applies 75%   Applies somewhat 20%

9. As adults, many of us misidentifed the role of sex in relationships, attempting to use sex to avoid abandonment, control others, or fill our emptiness.

   Definitely applies 87%   Applies somewhat 9%

10. As adults, many of us confused sex with emotional intimacy.

    Definitely applies 83%   Applies somewhat 12%

Incidence of Sex Addiction in ACSD Members Childhood Families

My father	75.0%
My mother	37.5
At least one of my siblings	33.3
My father's father	20.8
My mother's father	16.6
My father's mother	8.3
My mother's mother	4.2

The total percentages add up to more than 100 because some people thought that more than one person in their families were sexually addicted.

Marital Status of ACSD Members and the General Population of Minnesota

	ACSD Members	Other Minnesotans
Never Married	50%	28.5%
Married or living together	32	58.5
Divorced	14	5
Separated	5	1

Since our society does not yet allow gay men and lesbians officially to marry, their responses were not included in this table, and the figures are corrected for sexual preference. An additional 7 percent of the general population of Minnesota was single, owing to the death of spouses. The general population of Minnesota was used as a comparison group since, at the time the information on ACSD was gathered, all of the members resided in Minnesota. The figures on Minnesotans were gathered by the U.S. Census and obtained from the Minnesota Data Book (1986).

ACSD Members' History of Attending Other Twelve Step Groups

Sex Addicts Anonymous	79.0%
Al-Anon	50
Overeaters Anonymous	33.3
Alcoholics Anonymous	29
Adult Children of Alcoholics	25
Children of Sex Addicts Anonymous	12.5
Sex and Love Addicts Anonymous	12.5
Narcotics Anonymous	12.5
Emotions Anonymous	8.3
Sexaholics Anonymous	4
Overeaters Anonymous	4
Debtors Anonymous	4
Adults Recovering from Incest Anonymous	4

The total percentages add up to more than 100 because some people had attended more than one type of recovery group.

Members' Current Attendance in Other Twelve Step Meetings

None	37.5%
Sex Addicts Anonymous	33.3
Al-Anon	12.5
Overeaters Anonymous	12.5
Alcoholics Anonymous	4
Adult Children of Alcoholics	4
Adults Recovering from Incest Anonymous	4

Resources

How to Reach Mutual-help Groups

Adult Children of Sexual Dysfunction, P.O. Box 8084, Lake Street Station, 110 East 31st Street, Minneapolis, Minnesota 55408.
(If you would like information, please enclose a legal-size, self-addressed, *stamped* envelope.)

Codependents of Sex Addicts (CoSA), P.O. Box 14537, Minneapolis, Minnesota 55414, (612) 537-6904. Please include a self-addressed, *stamped* envelope.

Incest Survivors Anonymous (ISA), P.O. Box 5613, Long Beach, California 90805, (213) 422-1632.

Sexaholics Anonymous (SA), P.O. Box 300, Simi Valley, California 93062, (818) 704-9854.

S-Anon, P.O. Box 5117, Sherman Oaks, California 91413, (818) 990-6910.

Sex Addicts Anonymous (SAA), P.O. Box 3038, Minneapolis, Minnesota 55403, (612) 871-1520.

Books of Related Interest

Anonymous. *Hope and Recovery: A Twelve Step Guide to Healing From Compulsive Sexual Behavior.* Minneapolis: CompCare Publishers, 1987. Self-help book for sex addicts applies the Twelve Steps to this complex problem.

Anonymous. *Hope and Recovery.* Minneapolis: CompCare Publishers, 1988. A word-for-word audiotape of the first eighteen chapters from the groundbreaking book.

Anonymous. *Hope and Recovery: The Workbook.* Minneapolis: CompCare Publishers, 1990. Questions clarifying issues and drawing connections to the reader's life and experience.

Anonymous. *What Everyone Needs to Know About Sex Addiction.* Minneapolis: CompCare Publishers, 1989. Introduction to sex addiction, describing the problem and pointing the way toward recovery sources.

Carnes, Patrick. *Contrary to Love: Helping the Sex Addict.* Minneapolis: CompCare Publishers, 1989.

————. *Out of the Shadows: Understanding Sexual Addiction.* Minneapolis: CompCare Publishers, 1983.

Hunter, Mic. *Abused Boys: The Neglected Victims of Sexual Abuse.* Lexington, Mass.: Lexington Books, 1990; New York: Fawcett Books, 1991. For survivors of childhood sexual abuse and their partners.

Hunter, Mic, with "Jem." *The First Step: A Workbook for People in Relationships With Sex Addicts.* Minneapolis: CompCare Publishers, 1989. For persons who as adults find themselves in relationships with partners who are unfaithful, compulsively masturbate, collect pornography, use prostitutes, or are otherwise preoccupied with sex.

————. *Recovering From Shame Through the Twelve Steps*. Center City, Minn.: Hazelden Educational Materials, 1991. An audiotape of a presentation about using the Twelve Step program to heal from shame.

————, ed. *The Sexually Abused Male, Volume I: Prevalence, Impact and Treatment; Volume II: Application of Treatment Strategies.* Lexington, Mass.: Lexington Books, 1991. For treatment professionals who seek practical techniques for working with sexual abuse survivors of all ages.

————. *The Twelve Steps and Shame*. Center City, Minn.: Hazelden Foundation, 1988. Describes differences between guilt and shame. Overview of how the Twelve Step program can be used to heal a shame-based identity.

————. *What Is Sexual Addiction?* Center City, Minn.: Hazelden Foundation, 1988. Overview of sex addiction and some of the common characteristics.

LairRobinson, Barbara, with Rick LairRobinson. *If My Dad's a Sexaholic, What Does That Make Me?* Minneapolis: CompCare Publishers, 1991. Authoritative definition of family sex addiction, by therapists who are themselves adult children.

About the Author

Mic Hunter is licensed as both psychologist and marriage and family therapist and is a certified alcohol and drug counselor and chemical dependency counselor (reciprocal). His education includes a bachelor of arts degree in psychology from Macalester College, a master of arts degree in human development from Saint Mary's College Graduate Center, and a master of science degree in education and psychological services from the University of Wisconsin–Superior. He completed the two-year Intensive Post-graduate Training Program at the Gestalt Institute of the Twin Cities; and the University of Minnesota's Alcohol/Drug Counselor Education Program in the School of Public Health, and Chemical Dependency and Family Intimacy Training Project in the Program in Human Sexuality. He is currently a doctoral student in clinical psychology at the Minnesota School of Professional Psychology.

Mic works with adult children of sexually dysfunctional families in his private practice in St. Paul, Minnesota. He lives in St. Paul with his wife, Kate An.